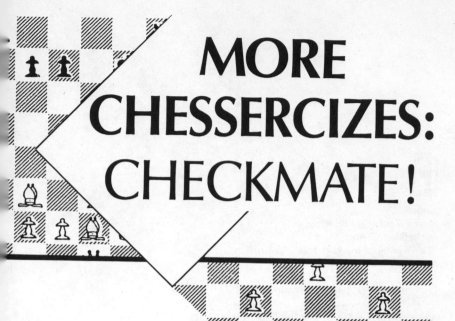

MORE CHESSERCIZES: CHECKMATE!

BRUCE PANDOLFINI

A FIRESIDE BOOK
Published by Simon & Schuster
NEW YORK   LONDON   TORONTO   SYDNEY   TOKYO   SINGAPORE

Fireside
Simon & Schuster Building
Rockefeller Center
1230 Avenue of the Americas
New York, New York 10020

Designed by Stanley S. Drate/Folio Graphics Co., Inc.
Manufactured in the United States of America

10 9 8 7 6 5 4 3 2 1 Pbk.

Library of Congress Cataloging-in-Publication Data

Pandolfini, Bruce.
   More chessercizes : checkmate! / Bruce Pandolfini.
      p. cm.
   "A Fireside book."
   1. Chess problems. I. Title.
GV1451.P36   1991
794.1'076—dc20   90-28286
                                                  CIP

ISBN 0-671-70185-1 Pbk.

ACKNOWLEDGMENTS

I would like to thank chess master Bruce Alberston, for his analysis, research and chessic advice; Burt Hochberg for copyediting the manuscript; Idelle Pandolfini, Carol Ann Caronia, Larry Tamarkin, Nick Conticello, Bonni Leon, Renée Rabb, Gypsy da Silva; and my editor Kara Leverte who was brilliant throughout, from concept to product.

For Joe,
who first introduced me
to the world of chess.

CONTENTS

INTRODUCTION

What's chess all about?

Quick answer: Get the enemy king as fast as you can. Effective aggression, or forcing mate in as few moves as possible, is the point.

Chessercizes: Checkmate! is a collection of three hundred problems, each of them a forced checkmate for you to discover. If you play a forced checkmate correctly, your opponent can't avoid losing, even with the best defense.

The examples are arranged in five chapters, each chapter increasing by one the number of moves required to force mate. Chapter One contains only mates in two, Chapter Two mates in three, and so on through Chapter Five, which offers mates in six and, finally, seven moves. A further ordering occurs within each chapter, where the easier problems come first and are followed by the harder ones.

Each problem is introduced by a directive. In Chapter One, "White mates in two" means that White moves first, Black responds, and White's second move is the stroke of mate. "Black mates in two" means that Black moves first, White answers, and Black then mates. Similarly, "White mates in three" means White goes first, Black responds, White and Black move again, and White mates on his third move.

The answers are provided in the last section. The main solution to each problem is set in boldface type. Alternative defenses are listed under the main solution in regular type. If there are many reasonable alternatives, several representative continuations are provided to show how corresponding defenses are handled.

All answers are given in algebraic notation, which is explained in the section following this introduction.

For the defender, the main-line defense is the one that lasts the longest: Surviving for four moves is better than losing in three. If several variations are equal in length, the main line is the most natural one, the one to be considered first.

To get the most from this book, try to solve the problems from the diagrammed positions without setting them up on a chessboard. This lets you practice visualizing chess moves in your head, which is what you do when actually playing. (Your opponents won't let you move the pieces around to see if your ideas really work!)

If you can't solve a problem after several minutes, then set up the position on an actual chessboard. But even with real pieces in front of you, you should still try to find the solution without moving anything. Only after you've tried to discover the right moves this way should you move the pieces. Simulate game conditions. Pretend it's against the rules to take a move back or to experiment with a variation to see if it works. This can help you develop your analytic skills and improve your play more quickly. No pain, no gain.

If you're not a born killer, you can learn how to be one in chess. Solving the checkmate exercises can sharpen your tactics and aggressive instincts while increasing your stockpile of patterns and related weapons. You learn the potential of the pieces individually and in combination with others. Progressing through *Chessercizes: Checkmate!*, you'll solve harder and deeper problems, expanding your capacity to see ahead and to exploit similar situations in your games.

Chessercizes: Checkmate! is based on situations that can occur in the opening or early middlegame of your actual games. Play through the book the first time for fun, noting how long it takes to solve each problem. On a second reading, try to beat your earlier record by solving each problem faster. Later, whenever you want to sharpen your play, try re-solving a few problems in *Chessercizes: Checkmate!* Ideally, you'll want to determine the answer instantly. Spotting patterns quickly is what distinguishes strong players, and practicing, in this way, with diagrams, is one of their secrets.

A WORD ON CHESS NOTATION

In order to read the solutions to the problems, you must know the algebraic system of chess notation. In the algebraic system:

- The *board* is an eight-by-eight grid of sixty-four squares.
- The *files* (the rows of squares going up the board) are lettered *a* through *h*, beginning from White's left.
- The *ranks* (the rows of squares going across the board) are numbered *1* through *8*, beginning from White's nearest row.

You can readily identify any square by combining a letter and a number, with the letter written first (see diagram A). For example, the square occupied by White's king in the original position is *e1*, while the original square for Black's

A

BLACK

a8	b8	c8	d8	e8	f8	g8	h8
a7	b7	c7	d7	e7	f7	g7	h7
a6	b6	c6	d6	e6	f6	g6	h6
a5	b5	c5	d5	e5	f5	g5	h5
a4	b4	c4	d4	e4	f4	g4	h4
a3	b3	c3	d3	e3	f3	g3	h3
a2	b2	c2	d2	e2	f2	g2	h2
a1	b1	c1	d1	e1	f1	g1	h1

WHITE

13

king is *e8*. All squares in the algebraic grid are named from White's standpoint.

If you have trouble visualizing diagram A, I suggest you make a photocopy of it, cut out the grid, and use it as a bookmark in this book. Thus it will always be handy when you need it, though after a while you probably won't need it at all. As a further reference, you will note that in this book the numbers and letters are conveniently arranged on the outside of each diagram. You should have no trouble understanding these diagrams and their corresponding solutions.

Symbols You Should Know

K	King
Q	Queen
R	Rook
B	Bishop
N	Knight
x	capture
+	check
+ +	checkmate
0–0	castles Kingside
0–0–0	castles Queenside
1.	White's first move
1. . . .	Black's first move (when appearing independently of White's)
2.	White's second move
2. . . .	Black's second move
Any	Any legal move

Reading the Solutions

Consider the shortest chess game possible. The four moves of this game are in Diagrams B through E.

14

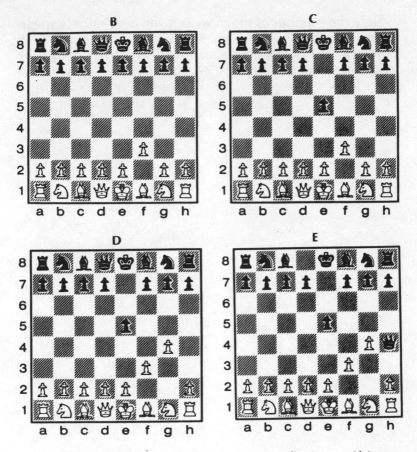

The game illustrated in the foregoing diagrams, if it appeared in the answer section, would look like this:

1. f3 e5   2. g4 Qh4 + +

1. f3	means that White's first move is pawn to f3.
e5	means that Black's response is pawn to e5.
2. g4	means that White's second move is pawn to g4.
Qh4 + +	means that Black's second move is queen to h4, mate.

15

Note the number of the move is given only once, appearing just before White's move. The correct answer is given in boldface, and interesting alternatives are given under the main line in regular type.

MORE CHESSERCIZES: CHECKMATE!

1

MATES IN TWO

Chapter One, problems 1–74, provides checkmates to be solved in two moves. In problems 1–36, 47, 56–63, and 71–74, White mates in two moves. This means White moves, Black moves, and White mates. Problems 37–46, 48–55, and 64–70 offer situations in which Black mates in two. Black therefore plays the first move, White responds, and Black mates.

A number of themes are encountered in Chapter One. Smothered mates occur in examples, 1, 14, and 54. In the minds of many, this mate, always given by a lone knight, is the most beautiful checkmate of all. Another pattern is the back-rank mate (12, 25, 38, and 48), where a rook or queen snares the enemy king along its first rank. Then there are mates based on pins (2, 5, 10, and 57), where a defending piece is prevented from guarding a key square. Discoveries also appear (19 and 59), where a piece moves out of the line of a friendly piece, unveiling the stationary piece's attack. If both the stationary and moving units give check, it is called double check, as in example 56.

One of the most frequently seen checkmates in this chapter is the memorable criss-cross mate. It occurs when the attacking diagonals of two friendly bishops or bishop and queen cross in the mating pattern. Examples, 3, 6, 20, 23, 45, 46, 53, 58, 62, and 69 hinge on this popular theme.

1

White mates in 2 moves

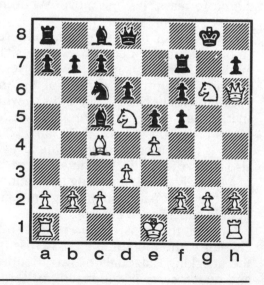

2

White mates in 2 moves

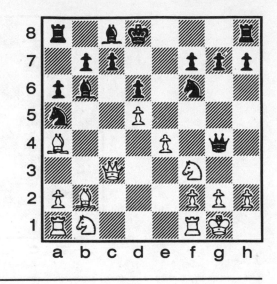

3

White mates in 2 moves

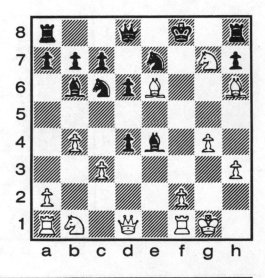

4

White mates in 2 moves

5

White mates in 2 moves

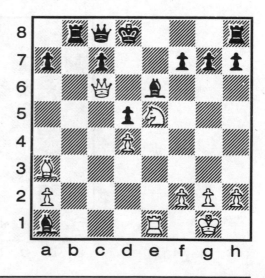

6

White mates in 2 moves

7

White mates in 2 moves

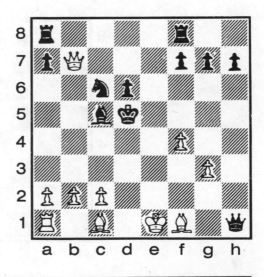

8

White mates in 2 moves

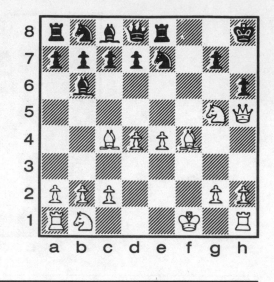

9

White mates in 2 moves

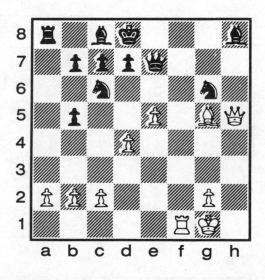

10

White mates in 2 moves

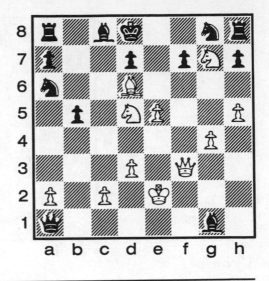

11

White mates in 2 moves

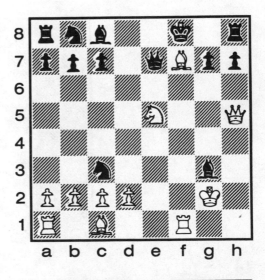

12

White mates in 2 moves

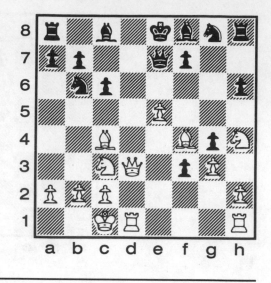

13

White mates in 2 moves

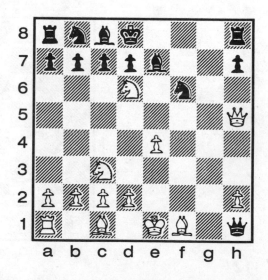

14

White mates in 2 moves

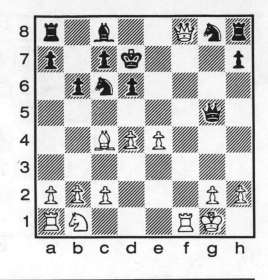

15

White mates in 2 moves

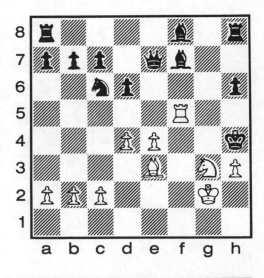

16

White mates in 2 moves

17

White mates in 2 moves

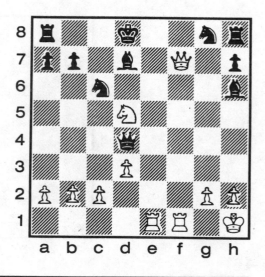

18

White mates in 2 moves

28

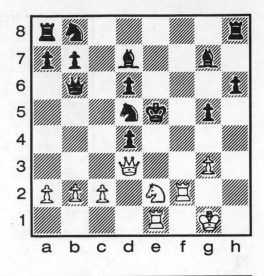

19

White mates in 2 moves

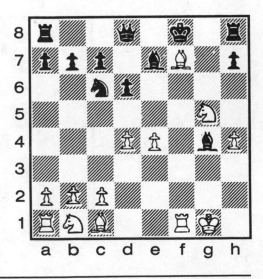

20

White mates in 2 moves

21

White mates in 2 moves

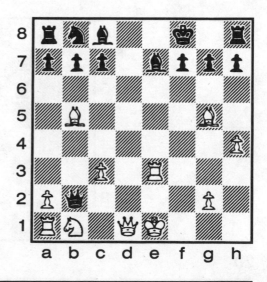

22

White mates in 2 moves

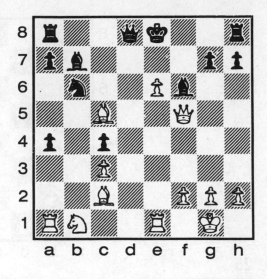

23

White mates in 2 moves

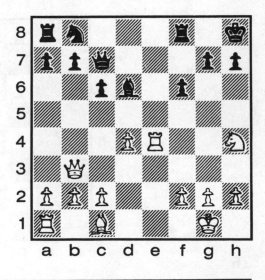

24

White mates in 2 moves

25

White mates in 2 moves

26

White mates in 2 moves

27

White mates in 2 moves

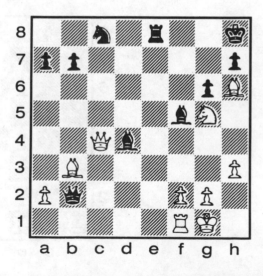

28

White mates in 2 moves

29

White mates in 2 moves·

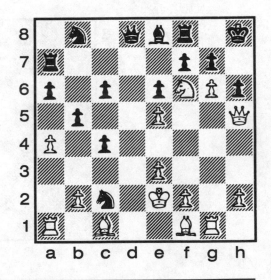

30

White mates in 2 moves

31

White mates in 2 moves

32

White mates in 2 moves

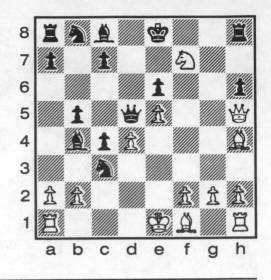

33

White mates in 2 moves

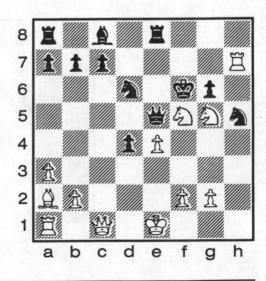

34

White mates in 2 moves

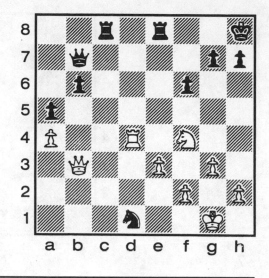

35

White mates in 2 moves

36

White mates in 2 moves

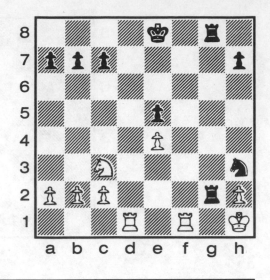

37

Black mates in 2 moves

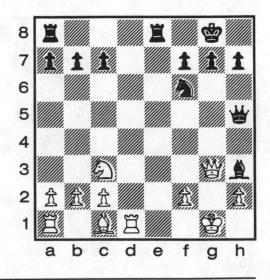

38

Black mates in 2 moves

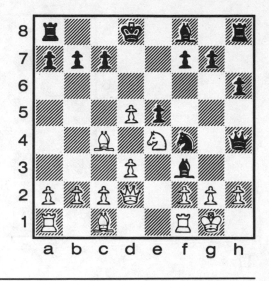

39

Black mates in 2 moves

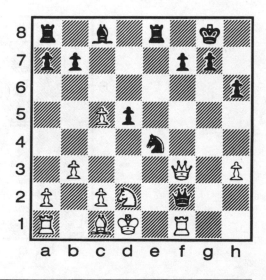

40

Black mates in 2 moves

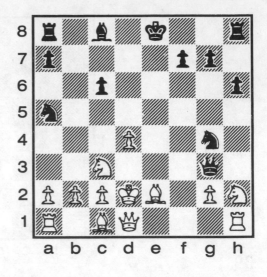

41

Black mates in 2 moves

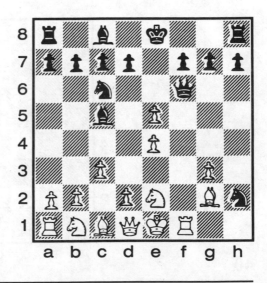

42

Black mates in 2 moves

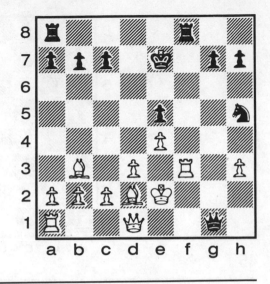

43

Black mates in 2 moves

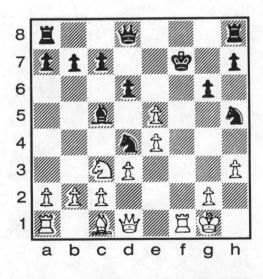

44

Black mates in 2 moves

45

Black mates in 2 moves

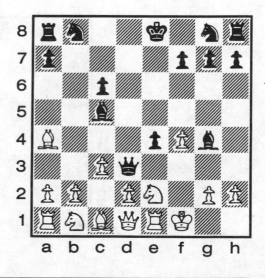

46

Black mates in 2 moves

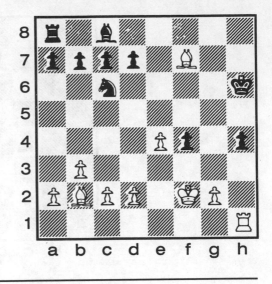

47

Black mates in 2 moves

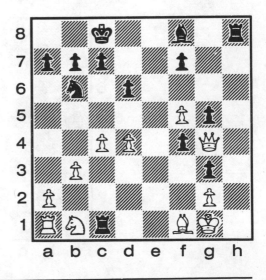

48

Black mates in 2 moves

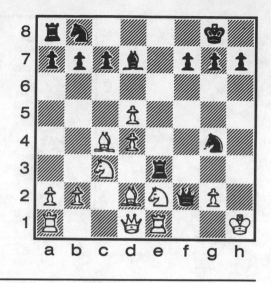

49

Black mates in 2 moves

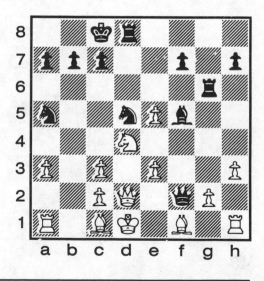

50

Black mates in 2 moves

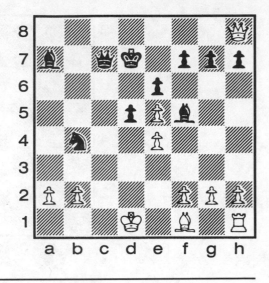

51

Black mates in 2 moves

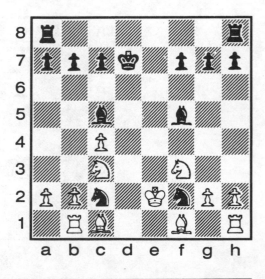

52

Black mates in 2 moves

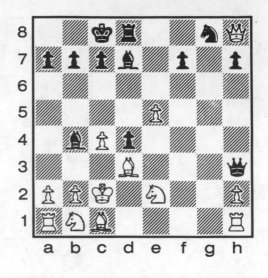

53

Black mates in 2 moves

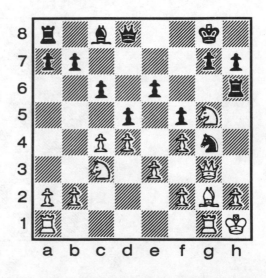

54

Black mates in 2 moves

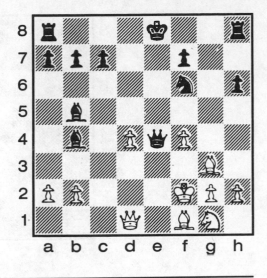

55

Black mates in 2 moves

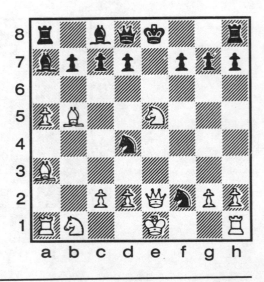

56

White mates in 2 moves

57

White mates in 2 moves

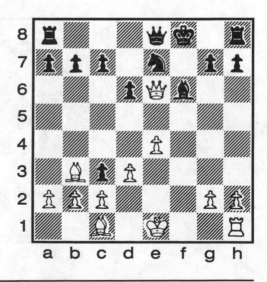

58

White mates in 2 moves

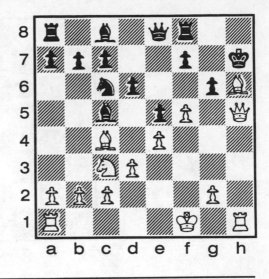

59

White mates in 2 moves

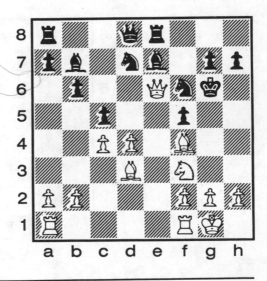

60

White mates in 2 moves

61

White mates in 2 moves

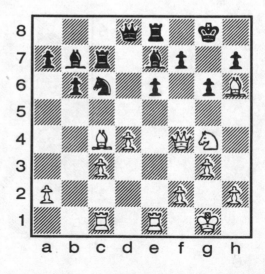

62

White mates in 2 moves

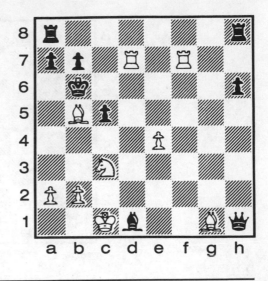

63

White mates in 2 moves

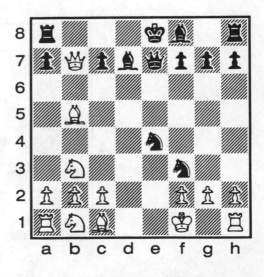

64

Black mates in 2 moves

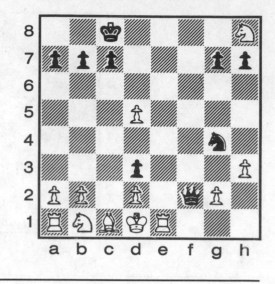

65

Black mates in 2 moves

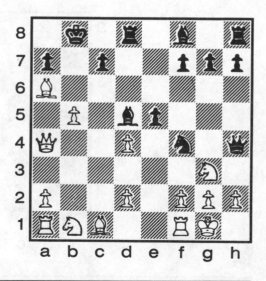

66

Black mates in 2 moves

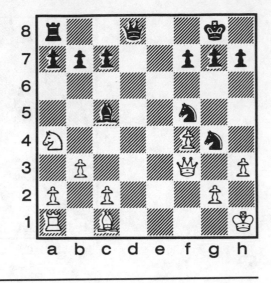

67

Black mates in 2 moves

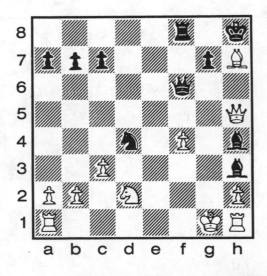

68

Black mates in 2 moves

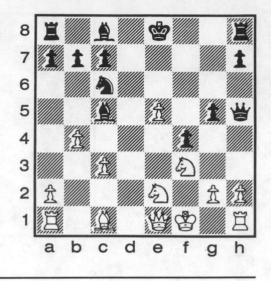

69

Black mates in 2 moves

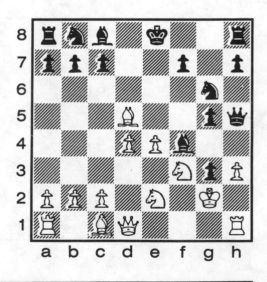

70

Black mates in 2 moves

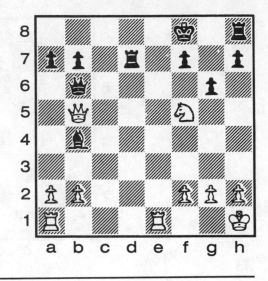

71

White mates in 2 moves

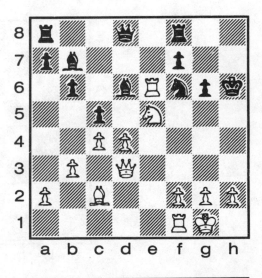

72

White mates in 2 moves

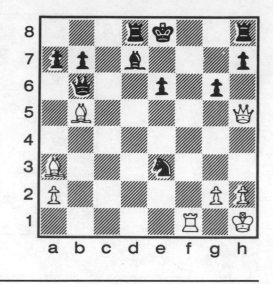

73

White mates in 2 moves

74

White mates in 2 moves

2

MATES IN THREE

Chapter Two, the longest of the book's five chapters, offers 100 checkmates in three moves, examples 75–174. White mates in three moves in problems 75–133, 163–164, 169, and 173–174. Black mates in three moves in problems 134–162, 165–168, and 170–172.

"White mates in three" means that White moves first, Black responds, White moves again, Black responds again, and White mates. "Black mates in three" means Black goes first and mates on his third move.

Generally, mates in three are harder to solve than mates in two because you must see an extra move ahead. Some of the prominent patterns in this chapter are mates on the back rank by a rook supported by a bishop (these are sometimes called support mates). Examples 103, 105, 109, 123, 132, and 150 illustrate this motif. Another recurring idea is to set up a discovered check by a queen sacrifice. Problems 78, 100, 112, 122, 124, and 134 display the raw power of such stratagems.

Many of the positions are related. Diagrams 81 and 85, for example, highlight the same one-two punch from cooperating knights, while diagrams 97 and 98 are obviously variations on the same opening trap.

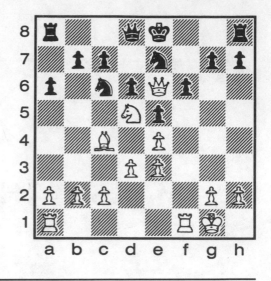

75

White mates in 3 moves

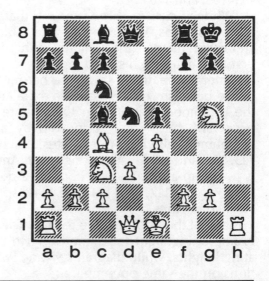

76

White mates in 3 moves

77

White mates in 3 moves

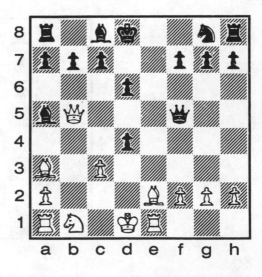

78

White mates in 3 moves

79

White mates in 3 moves

80

White mates in 3 moves

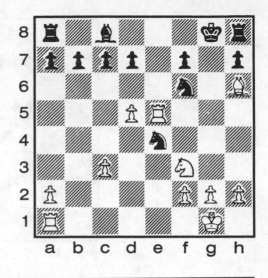

81

White mates in 3 moves

82

White mates in 3 moves

83

White mates in 3 moves

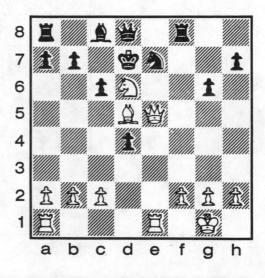

84

White mates in 3 moves

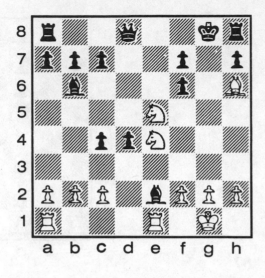

85

White mates in 3 moves

86

White mates in 3 moves

87

White mates in 3 moves

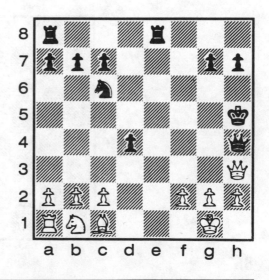

88

White mates in 3 moves

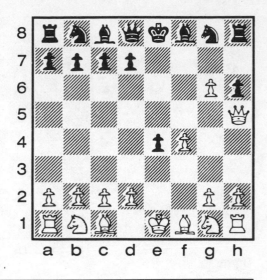

89

White mates in 3 moves

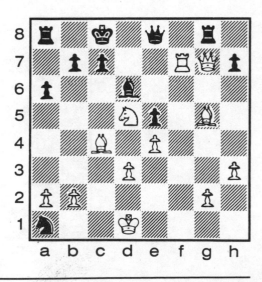

90

White mates in 3 moves

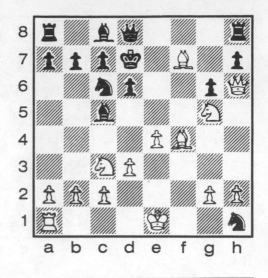

91

White mates in 3 moves

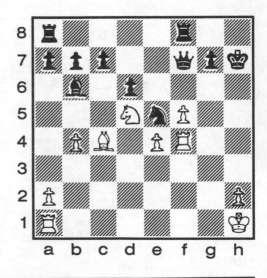

92

White mates in 3 moves

93

White mates in 3 moves

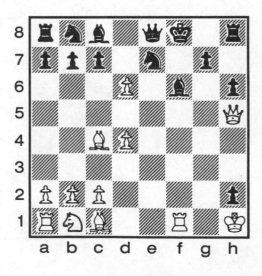

94

White mates in 3 moves

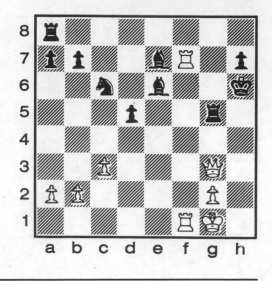

95

White mates in 3 moves

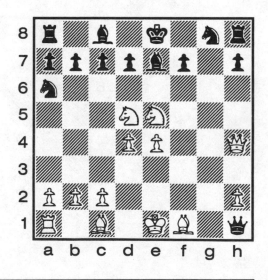

96

White mates in 3 moves

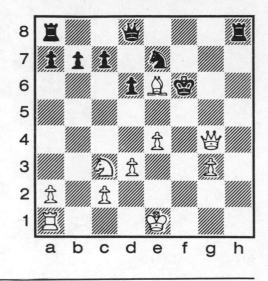

97

White mates in 3 moves

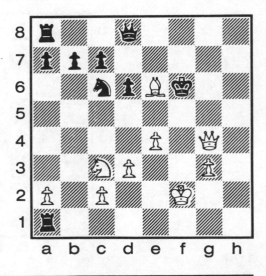

98

White mates in 3 moves

99

White mates in 3 moves

100

White mates in 3 moves

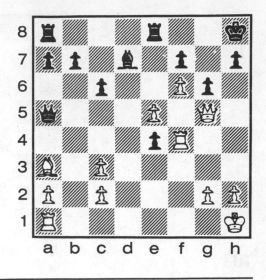

101

White mates in 3 moves

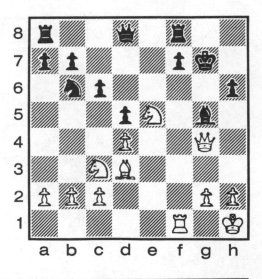

102

White mates in 3 moves

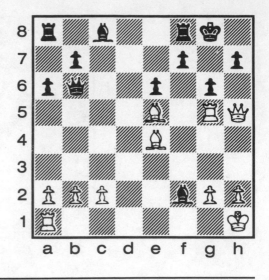

103

White mates in 3 moves

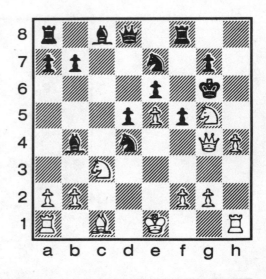

104

White mates in 3 moves

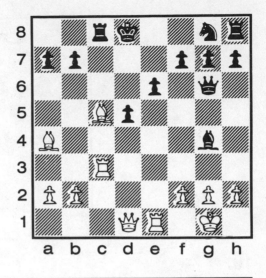

105

White mates in 3 moves

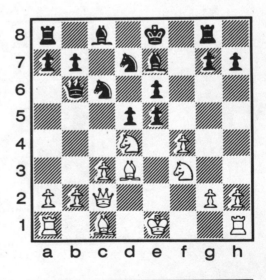

106

White mates in 3 moves

107

White mates in 3 moves

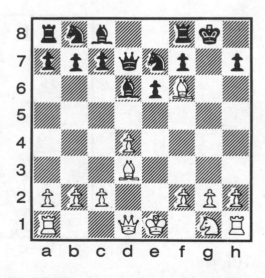

108

White mates in 3 moves

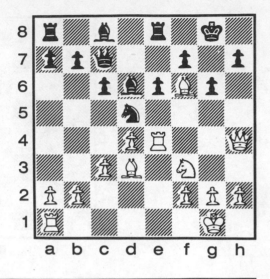

109

White mates in 3 moves

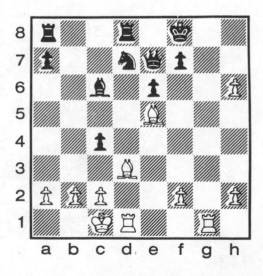

110

White mates in 3 moves

111

White mates in 3 moves

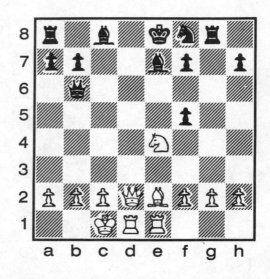

112

White mates in 3 moves

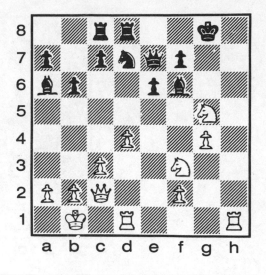

113

White mates in 3 moves

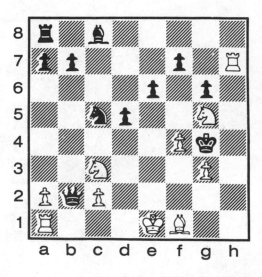

114

White mates in 3 moves

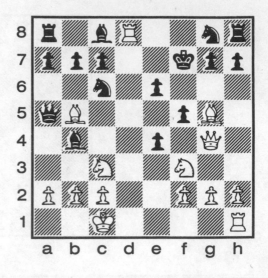

115

White mates in 3 moves

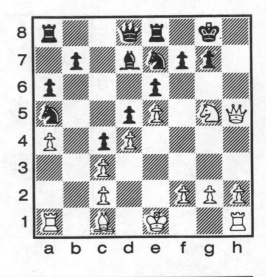

116

White mates in 3 moves

117

White mates in 3 moves

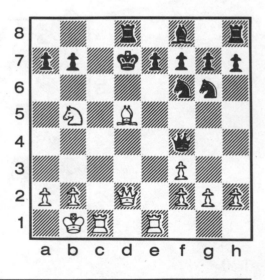

118

White mates in 3 moves

119

White mates in 3 moves

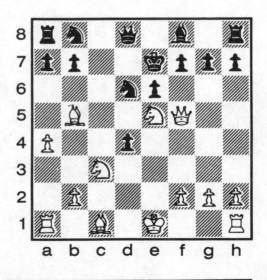

120

White mates in 3 moves

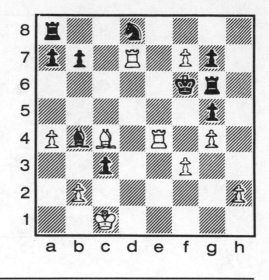

121

White mates in 3 moves

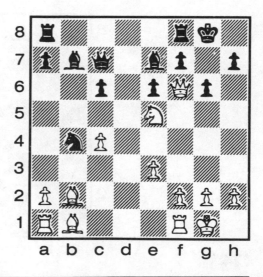

122

White mates in 3 moves

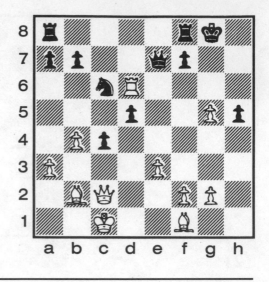

123

White mates in 3 moves

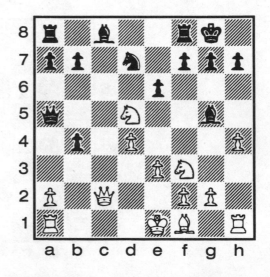

124

White mates in 3 moves

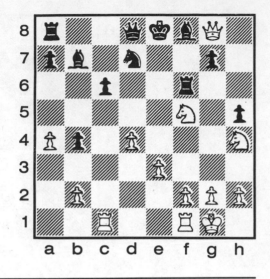

125

White mates in 3 moves

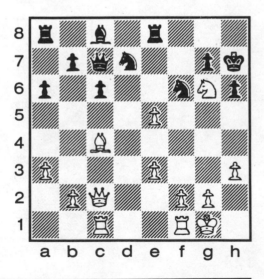

126

White mates in 3 moves

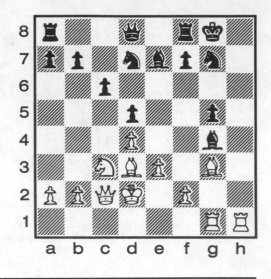

127

White mates in 3 moves

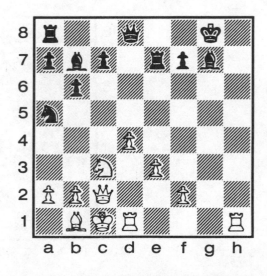

128

White mates in 3 moves

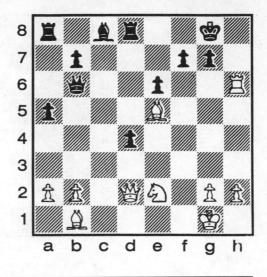

129

White mates in 3 moves

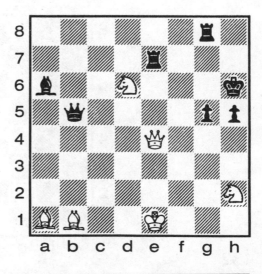

130

White mates in 3 moves

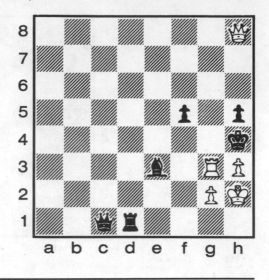

131

White mates in 3 moves

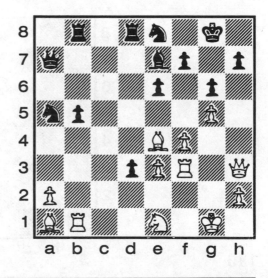

132

White mates in 3 moves

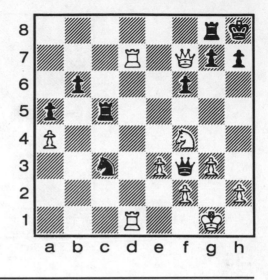

133

White mates in 3 moves

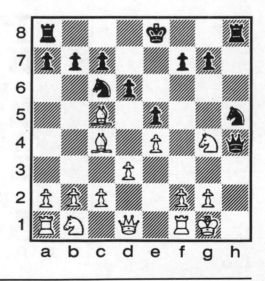

134

Black mates in 3 moves

135

Black mates in 3 moves

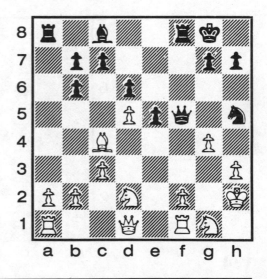

136

Black mates in 3 moves

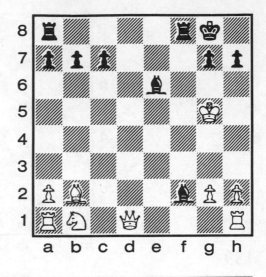

137

Black mates in 3 moves

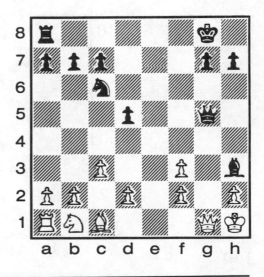

138

Black mates in 3 moves

139

Black mates in 3 moves

140

Black mates in 3 moves

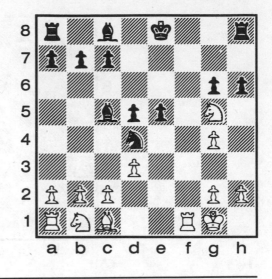

141

Black mates in 3 moves

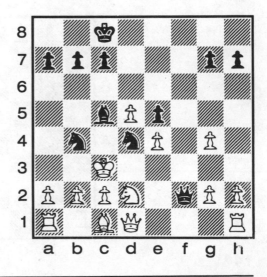

142

Black mates in 3 moves

143

Black mates in 3 moves

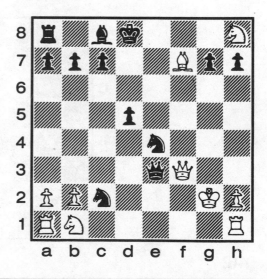

144

Black mates in 3 moves

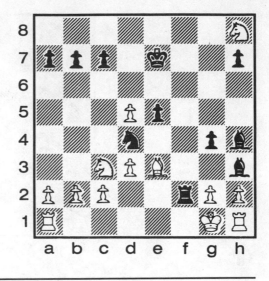

145

Black mates in 3 moves

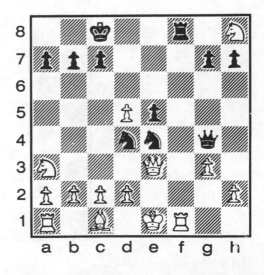

146

Black mates in 3 moves

147

Black mates in 3 moves

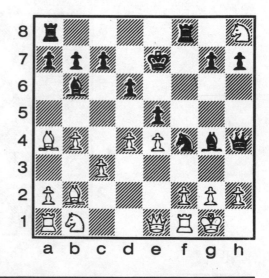

148

Black mates in 3 moves

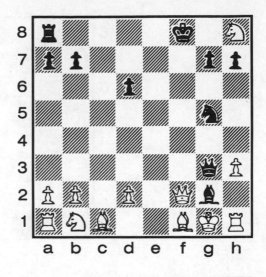

149

Black mates in 3 moves

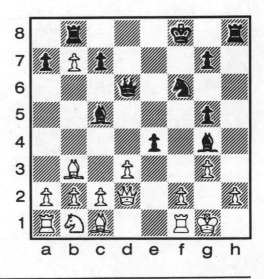

150

Black mates in 3 moves

151

Black mates in 3 moves

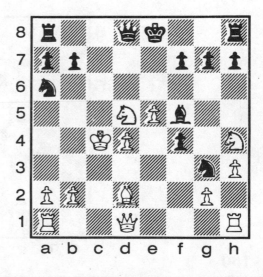

152

Black mates in 3 moves

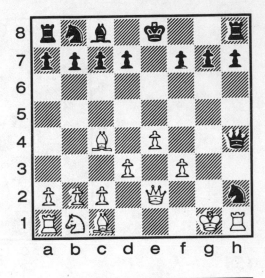

153

Black mates in 3 moves

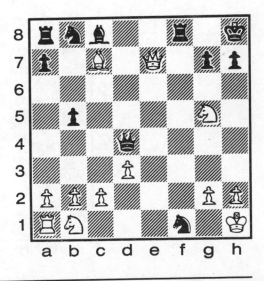

154

Black mates in 3 moves

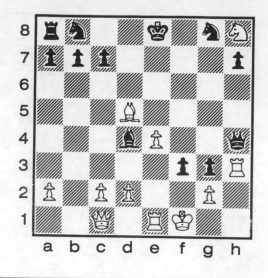

155

Black mates in 3 moves

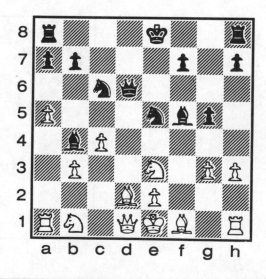

156

Black mates in 3 moves

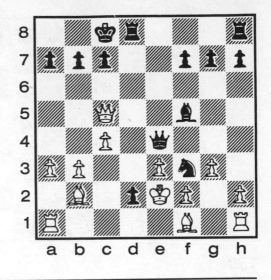

157

Black mates in 3 moves

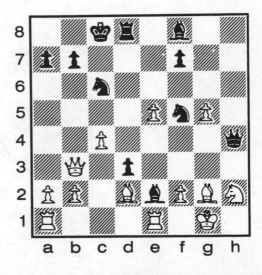

158

Black mates in 3 moves

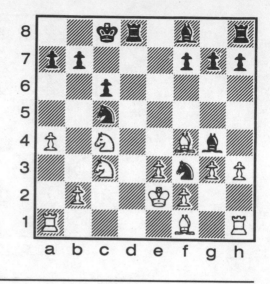

159

Black mates in 3 moves

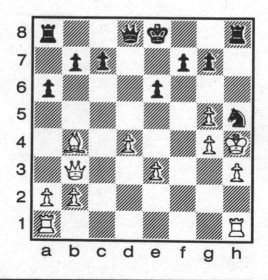

160

Black mates in 3 moves

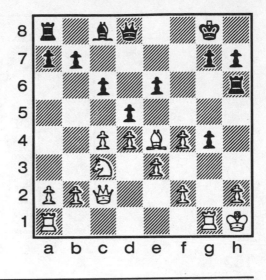

161

Black mates in 3 moves

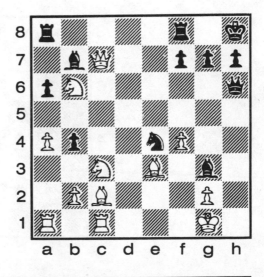

162

Black mates in 3 moves

163

Black mates in 3 moves

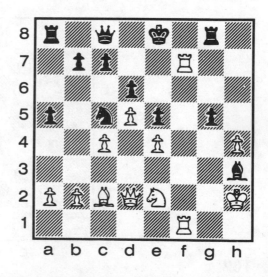

164

Black mates in 3 moves

165

Black mates in 3 moves

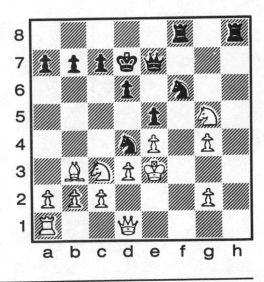

166

Black mates in 3 moves

167

Black mates in 3 moves

168

Black mates in 3 moves

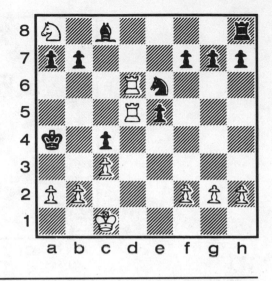

169

Black mates in 3 moves

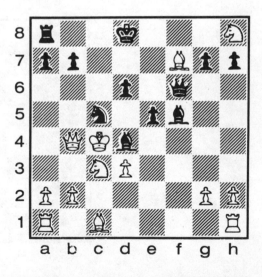

170

Black mates in 3 moves

171

Black mates in 3 moves

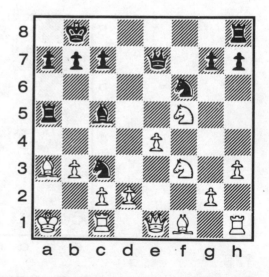

172

Black mates in 3 moves

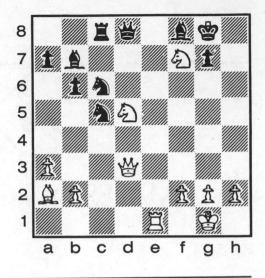

173

White mates in 3 moves

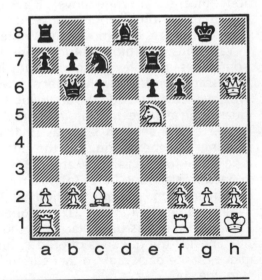

174

White mates in 3 moves

3

MATES IN FOUR

Chapter Three contains 58 checkmates in four moves, examples 175–232. White mates in four moves in diagrams 175–199, 216–222, and 228–231. Black mates in four moves in diagrams 200–215, 223–227, and 232. "White mates in four" means that White moves, Black responds, and so on, White mating on his fourth move. If "Black mates in four," then Black plays four moves and White plays three.

Variations get more intricate in this chapter, though sometimes a relatively simple mate is made longer—not necessarily harder—by the loser's delaying sacrifices. Noteworthy themes include the ability of the queen and rook to quard consecutive files as in examples 187 and 200; the power of the seventh rank, as in 188, 217, and 219; and chasing the enemy king up the board, driving it toward one's own forces, as in 209 and 212.

Sacrifices abound here: In 198 a rook is jettisoned so that the queen can get into position by giving check without wasting time; in 181 and 212 the queen is surrendered to remove protectors or obstacles to the enemy king; and in 183 and 193 the queen is offered to lure a blocking enemy piece off the back rank so that a friendly rook can deliver a winning check.

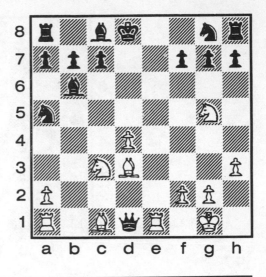

175

White mates in 4 moves

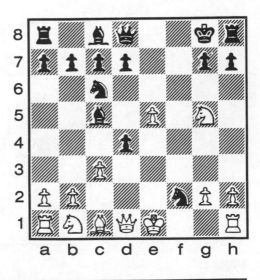

176

White mates in 4 moves

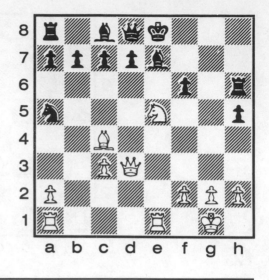

177

White mates in 4 moves

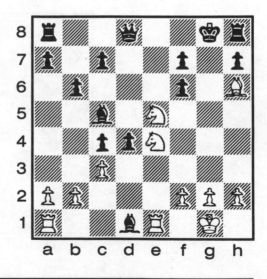

178

White mates in 4 moves

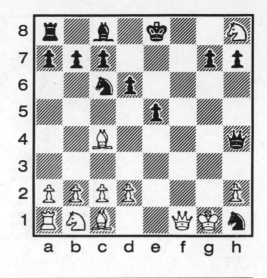

179

White mates in 4 moves

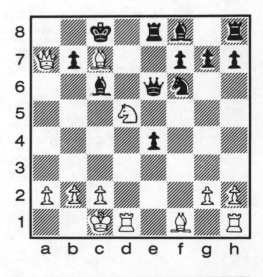

180

White mates in 4 moves

181

White mates in 4 moves

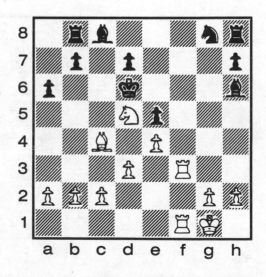

182

White mates in 4 moves

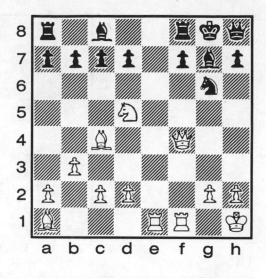

183

White mates in 4 moves

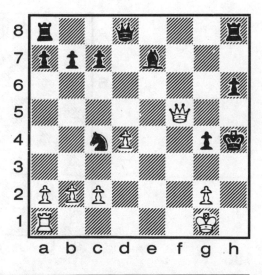

184

White mates in 4 moves

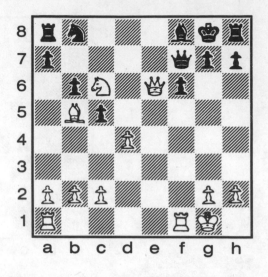

185

White mates in 4 moves

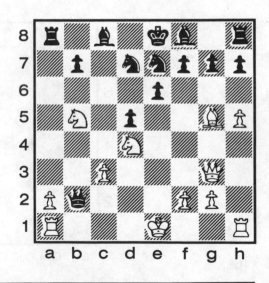

186

White mates in 4 moves

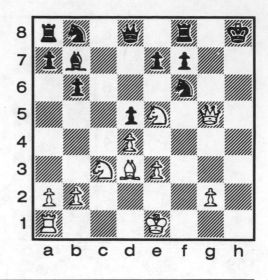

187

White mates in 4 moves

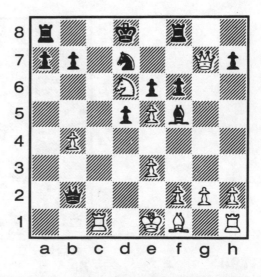

188

White mates in 4 moves

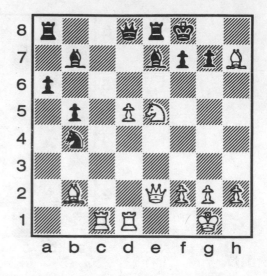

189

White mates in 4 moves

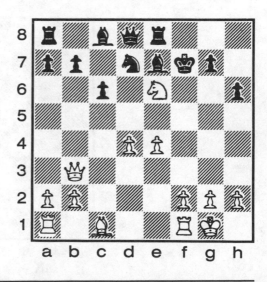

190

White mates in 4 moves

191

White mates in 4 moves

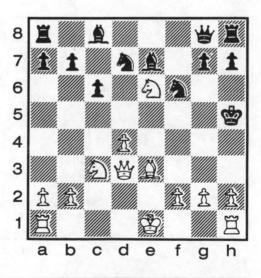

192

White mates in 4 moves

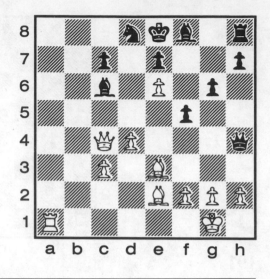

193

White mates in 4 moves

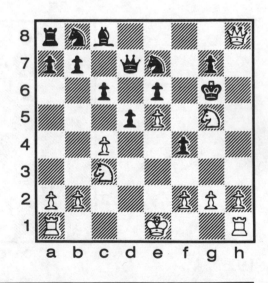

194

White mates in 4 moves

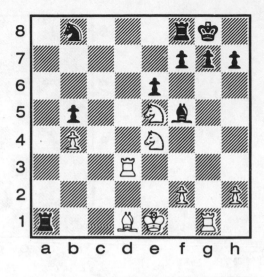

195

White mates in 4 moves

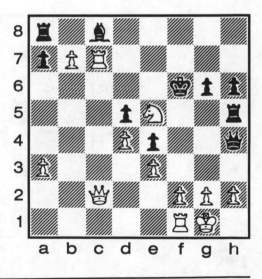

196

White mates in 4 moves

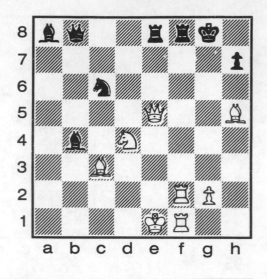

197

White mates in 4 moves

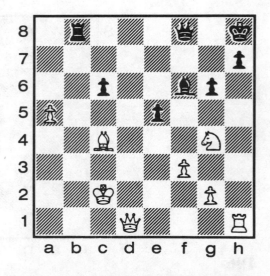

198

White mates in 4 moves

199

White mates in 4 moves

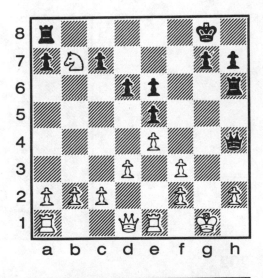

200

Black mates in 4 moves

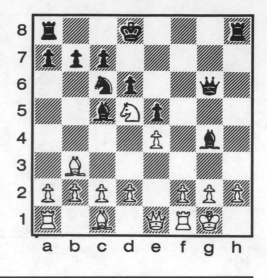

201

Black mates in 4 moves

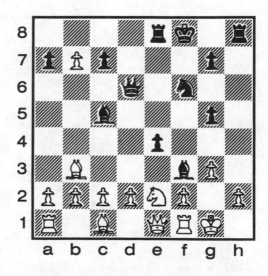

202

Black mates in 4 moves

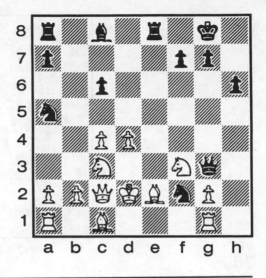

203

Black mates in 4 moves

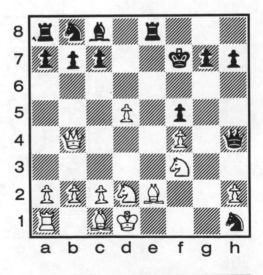

204

Black mates in 4 moves

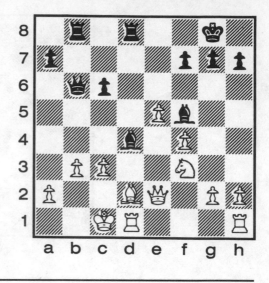

205

Black mates in 4 moves

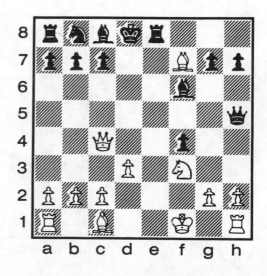

206

Black mates in 4 moves

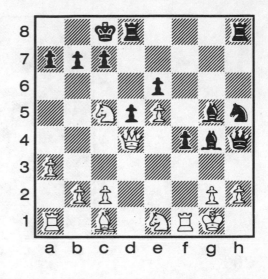

207

Black mates in 4 moves

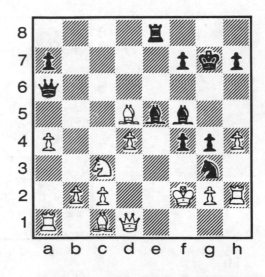

208

Black mates in 4 moves

209

Black mates in 4 moves

210

Black mates in 4 moves

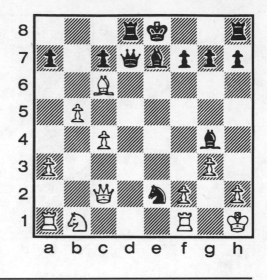

211

Black mates in 4 moves

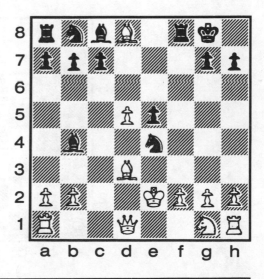

212

Black mates in 4 moves

213

Black mates in 4 moves

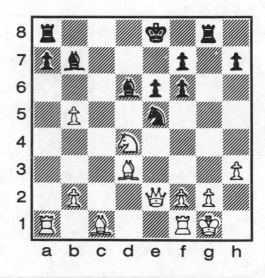

214

Black mates in 4 moves

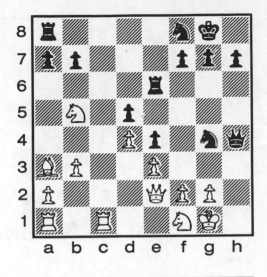

215

Black mates in 4 moves

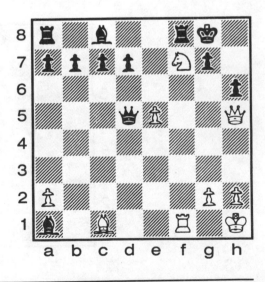

216

White mates in 4 moves

217

White mates in 4 moves

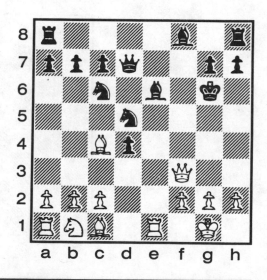

218

White mates in 4 moves

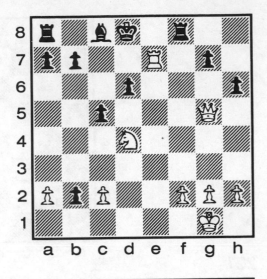

219

White mates in 4 moves

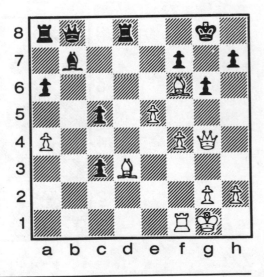

220

White mates in 4 moves

221

White mates in 4 moves

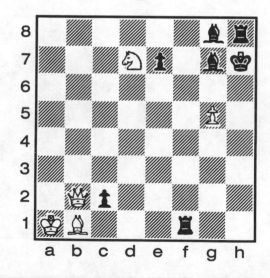

222

White mates in 4 moves

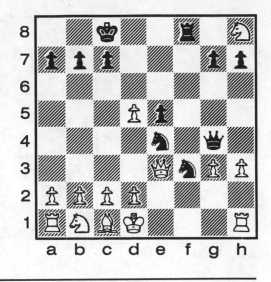

223

Black mates in 4 moves

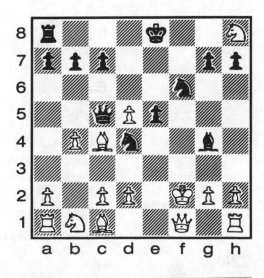

224

Black mates in 4 moves

133

225

Black mates in 4 moves

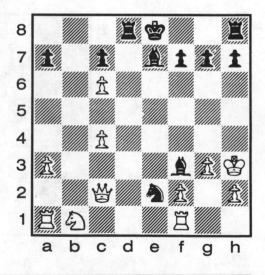

226

Black mates in 4 moves

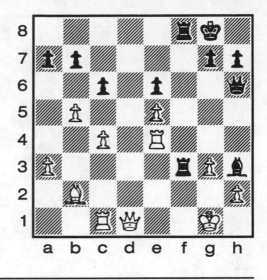

227

Black mates in 4 moves

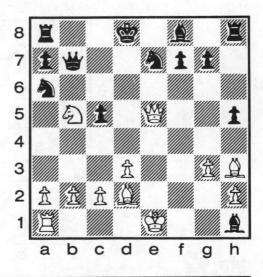

228

White mates in 4 moves

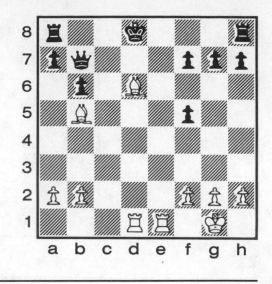

229

White mates in 4 moves

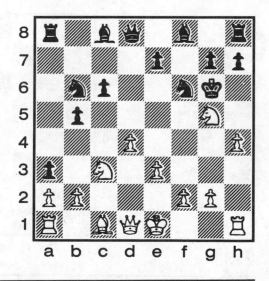

230

White mates in 4 moves

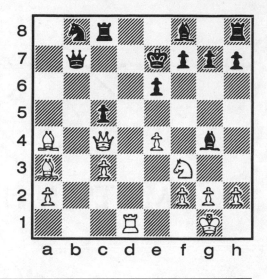

231

White mates in 4 moves

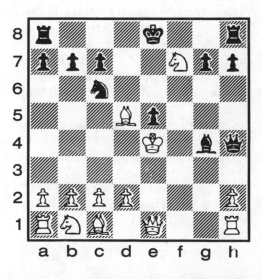

232

Black mates in 4 moves

4

MATES IN FIVE

Chapter Four presents 42 mates in five moves, examples 233–274. White mates in five moves in problems 233–256, 262–266, and 270–274. Black mates in five moves in 257–261 and 267–269.

One old favorite to look for is the Arabian Mate (example 237), in which a rook, supported by a knight that also guards an escape square, mates the enemy king, usually along the board's edge. The conclusions to examples 249 and 252 stem from classic bishop sacrifices, where the bishop is bait to lure out the enemy king and subject it to an avalanche of checks.

Checking sequences play an important role throughout the chapter. Consider the similarity between 262 and 272, both of which develop from the King's Gambit. Especially remember the finale, with White's bishop at c4 and queen at e5 combined in a beautiful mating pattern. Although a little different, example 263 shows a common link to the same kind of attack in the opening.

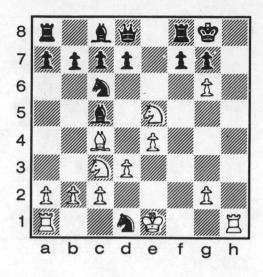

233

White mates in 5 moves

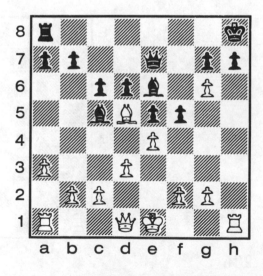

234

White mates in 5 moves

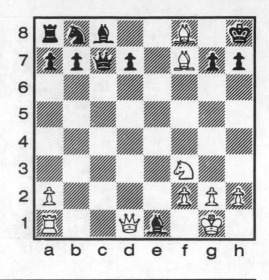

235

White mates in 5 moves

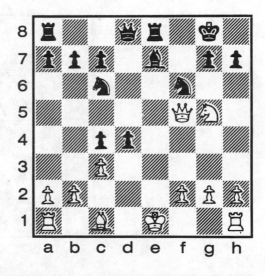

236

White mates in 5 moves

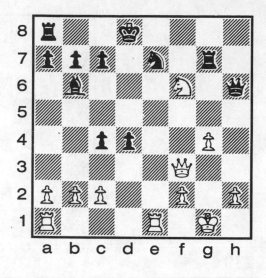

237

White mates in 5 moves

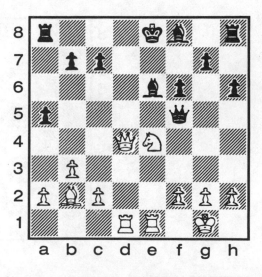

238

White mates in 5 moves

239

White mates in 5 moves

240

White mates in 5 moves

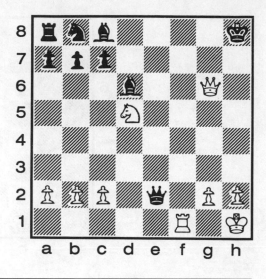

241

White mates in 5 moves

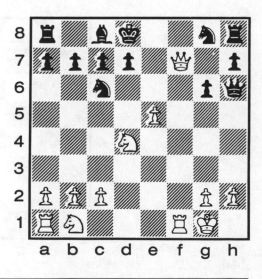

242

White mates in 5 moves

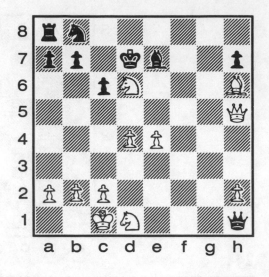

243

White mates in 5 moves

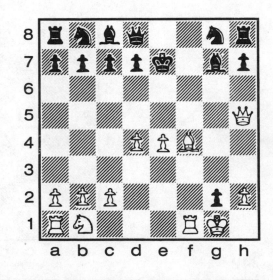

244

White mates in 5 moves

245

White mates in 5 moves

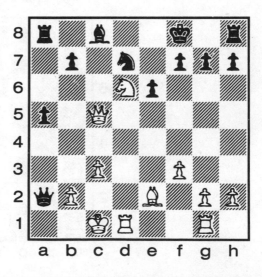

246

White mates in 5 moves

247

White mates in 5 moves

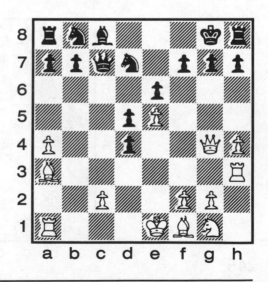

248

White mates in 5 moves

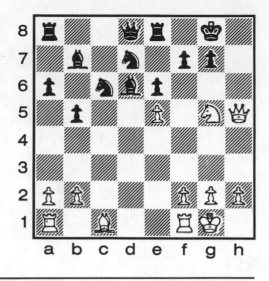

249

White mates in 5 moves

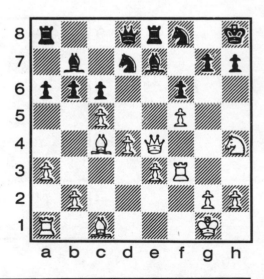

250

White mates in 5 moves

251

White mates in 5 moves

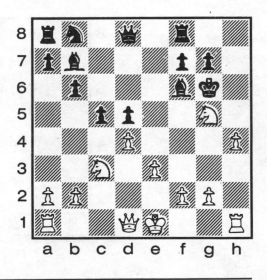

252

White mates in 5 moves

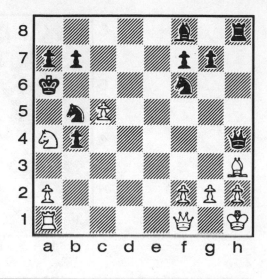

253

White mates in 5 moves

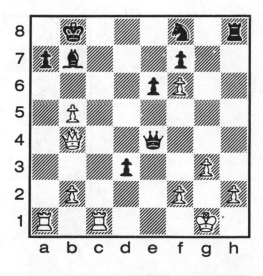

254

White mates in 5 moves

255

White mates in 5 moves

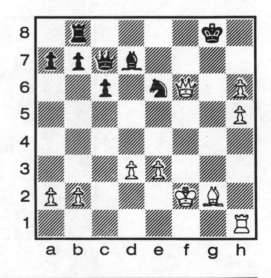

256

White mates in 5 moves

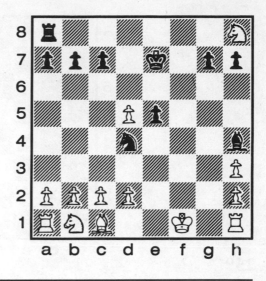

257

Black mates in 5 moves

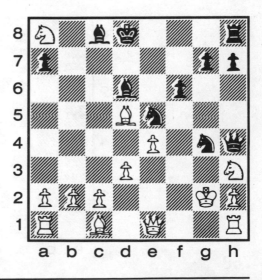

258

Black mates in 5 moves

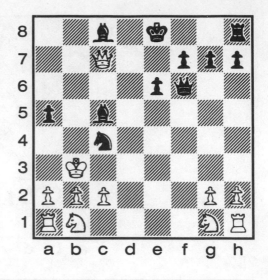

259

Black mates in 5 moves

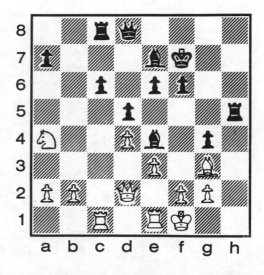

260

Black mates in 5 moves

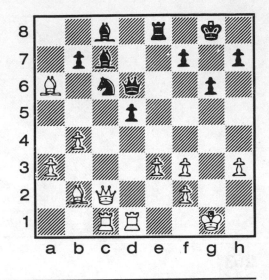

261

Black mates in 5 moves

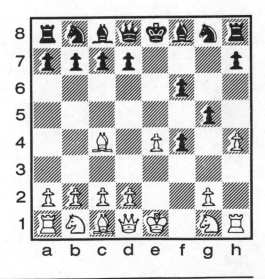

262

White moves in 5 moves

263

White moves in 5 moves

264

White moves in 5 moves

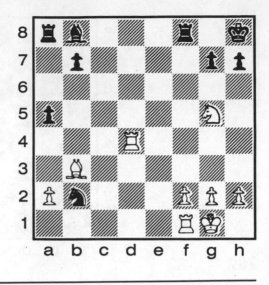

265

White moves in 5 moves

266

White moves in 5 moves

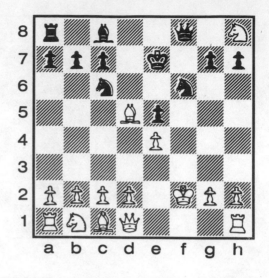

267

Black mates in 5 moves

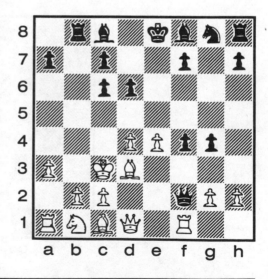

268

Black mates in 5 moves

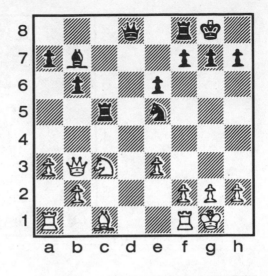

269

Black mates in 5 moves

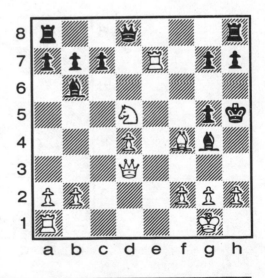

270

White mates in 5 moves

271

White mates in 5 moves

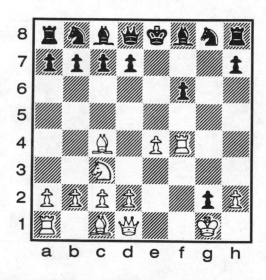

272

White mates in 5 moves

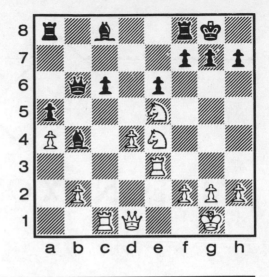

273

White mates in 5 moves

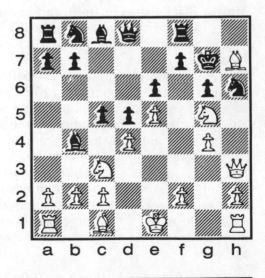

274

White mates in 5 moves

5

MATES IN SIX OR MORE

In Chapter Five, the last chapter of the book, twenty-six problems are offered for your pleasure, examples 275–300. White mates in six moves in 275–282, 288, and 296–297. Black mates in six moves in 283–287 and 289–295. The last three problems, examples 298–300, show mates in seven moves. Black mates in seven moves in 298–299, and White mates in seven moves in example 300.

Some variations in this final chapter are complicated. In addition to the correct line, we usually give the most typical secondary variations, especially in cases in which the defender must respond to nonchecking or nonforcing moves. If you think of an interesting move not given in the answers, play over the solution to see if any of the variations suggest the right reply to your move.

Among the more noteworthy positions is 280, where two Black queens are unable to stave off mate; examples 280 and 281, where bishop sacrifices on f7 lead to a series of pursuit checks against the uncastled Black king; and 276, which illustrates an unforgettable king hunt, the harried king driven across the board and eventually mated along the edge.

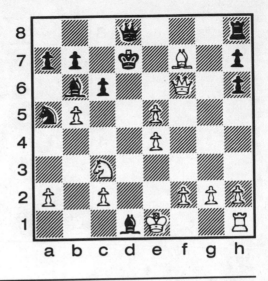

275

White mates in 6 moves

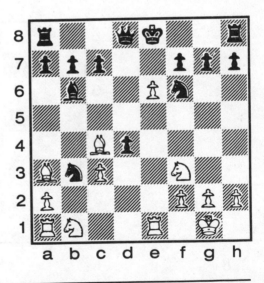

276

White mates in 6 moves

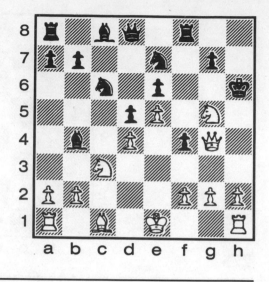

277

White mates in 6 moves

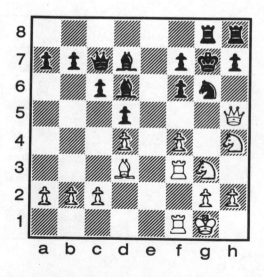

278

White mates in 6 moves

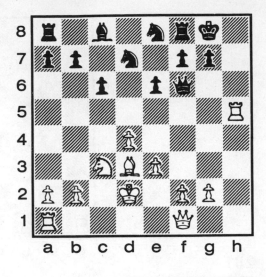

279

White mates in 6 moves

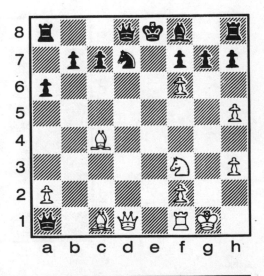

280

White mates in 6 moves

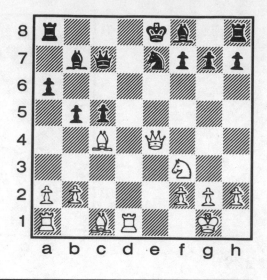

281

White mates in 6 moves

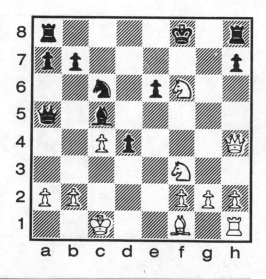

282

White mates in 6 moves

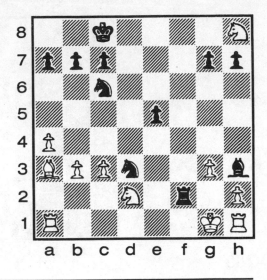

283

Black mates in 6 moves

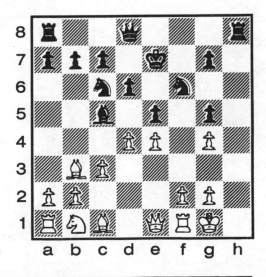

284

Black mates in 6 moves

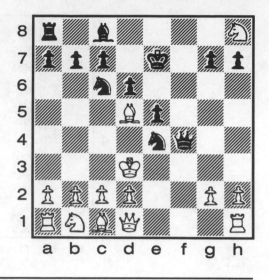

285

Black mates in 6 moves

286

Black mates in 6 moves

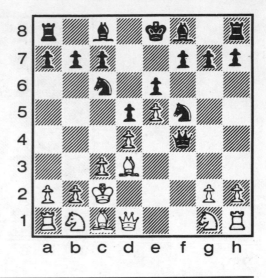

287

Black mates in 6 moves

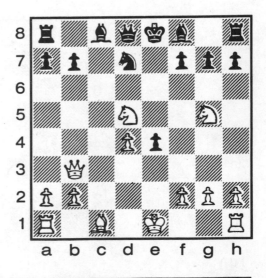

288

White mates in 6 moves

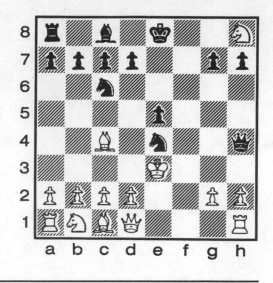

289

Black mates in 6 moves

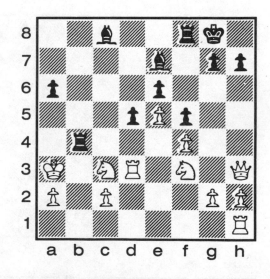

290

Black mates in 6 moves

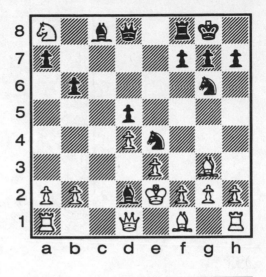

291

Black mates in 6 moves

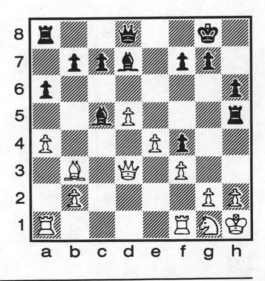

292

Black mates in 6 moves

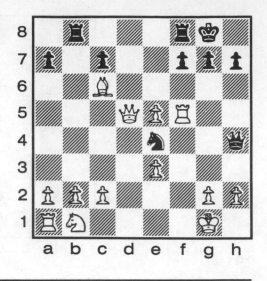

293

Black mates in 6 moves

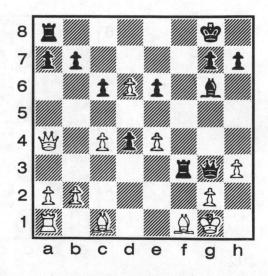

294

Black mates in 6 moves

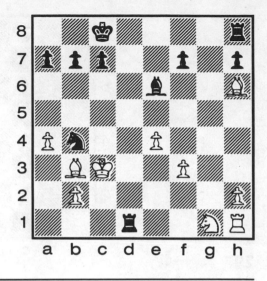

295

Black mates in 6 moves

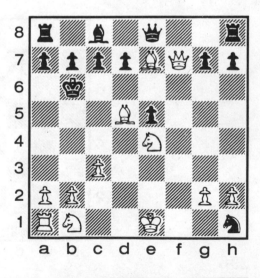

296

White mates in 6 moves

297

White mates in 6 moves

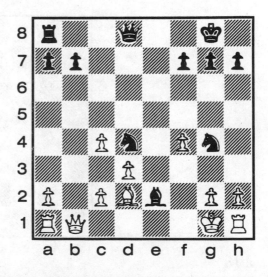

298

Black mates in 7 moves

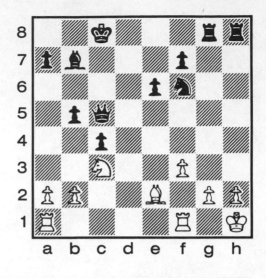

299

Black mates in 7 moves

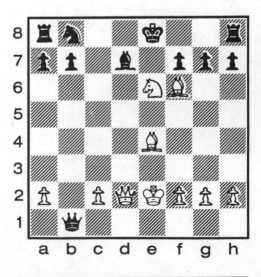

300

White mates in 7 moves

ANSWERS

CHAPTER ONE: MATES IN TWO

1) **1. Qg8+ R×g8 2. Nf7++**
2) **1. N×f6+ Q×f6 2. Qf8++**
3) **1. Q×f6+ g×f6 2. B×f6++**
4) **1. Nh5+ Ke8 2. Nf6++**
5) **1. Q×f7+ R×f7 2. Re8++**
6) **1. N×f7+ B×f7 2. Be7++**
7) **1. Q×f8+ N×f8 2. Re8++**
8) **1. Qb3+ Kd4 2. Qd3++**
      (or 1. . . . Ke4 2. Qd3++)
9) **1. Q×h6+ g×h6 2. Be5++**
10) **1. Q×h8+ N×h8 2. Rf8++**
      (or 1. . . . Nf8 2. R×f8++ or 2. Q×f8++)
11) **1. Qf6+ N×f6 2. Be7++**
      (or 1. . . . Ne7 2. B×e7++ or 2. Q×e7++)
12) **1. Ng6+ h×g6 2. Q×h8++**
13) **1. B×f7+ Q×f7 2. Qd8++**
      (or 1. . . . K×f7 2. Qg6++)
14) **1. Qe8+ R×e8 2. Nf7++**
      (or 1. . . . N×e8 2. Nf7++)
15) **1. Be6+ K×e6 2. Qf7++**
16) **1. Rh5+ B×h5 2. Nf5++**
17) **1. Qf5+ N×f5 2. e6++**
      (or 1. . . . Ne6 2. Q×e6++)
18) **1. Re8+ B×e8 2. Qc7++**
19) **1. Qe4+ K×e4 2. Nc3++**
20) **1. Ne6+ B×e6 2. Bh6++**
21) **1. Bf6+ N×f6 2. e×f6++**
22) **1. Qd8+ B×d8 2. Re8++**
23) **1. Qg6+ h×g6 2. B×g6++**

24) **1. Ng6+   h×g6   2. Rh3++**
25) **1. Bb6+   b×b6   2. R×e8++**
26) **1. Q×h7+   R×h7   2. Ng6++**
       (or   1. . . . Kf8   2. Ng6++ or   2. Qf7++)
27) **1. Nc6+   Ke8   2. Nc7++**
28) **1. Qg8+   R×g8   2. Nf7++**
29) **1. R×c4+   Q×c4   2. N×a7++**
30) **1. Q×h6+   g×h6   2. g7++**
31) **1. Rf8+   K×f8   2. Qf7++**
32) **1. Q×f7+   N×f7   2. Ng6++**
33) **1. Nd8+   Kd7   2. Qf7++**
       (or   1. . . . Kf8   2. Qf7++)
34) **1. Rf7+   N×f7   2. Nh7++**
35) **1. Ng6+   h×g6   2. Rh3++**
36) **1. Ng6+   h×g6   2. Qh4++**
37) **1. . . . Rg1+   2. R×g1   Nf2++**
38) **1. . . . Q×d1+   2. N×d1   Re1++**
39) **1. . . . Qh3   2. g×h3   N×h3++**
       (or   2. g×f3   Qg2++)
40) **1. . . . Nc3+   2. Q×c3   Qe2++**
41) **1. . . . Nc4+   2. B×c4   Qe3++**
42) **1. . . . Q×f1+   2. B×f1   Nf3++**
43) **1. . . . Ng3+   2. R×g3   Qf2++**
44) **1. . . . Nf3+   2. Kh1   Ng3++**
45) **1. . . . Nc5+   2. d×c5   Bf5++**
46) **1. . . . Qf3+   2. g×f3   Bh3++**
47) **1. Bf6   h3   2. R×h3++**
       Other first moves for Black permit 2. R×h4++.
48) **1. . . . Rh1+   2. K×h1   R×f1++**
49) **1. . . . Rh3+   2. g×h3   Qh2++**
50) **1. . . . N×e3+   2. Q×e3   B×c2++**
51) **1. . . . Qc2+   2. Ke1   B×f2++**
52) **1. . . . Bd3+   2. Kd2   Be3++**
53) **1. . . . Q×d3+   2. K×d3   Bf5++**
54) **1. . . . R×h2+   2. Q×h2   N×f2++**
55) **1. . . . Be1+   2. Q×e1   Ng4++**
       (or   1. . . . Ng4+   2. Q×g4   Be1++)

56) **1. N×d7+   N×e2   2. Nf6++**
   (or   1. . . . Qe7   2. Q×e7++;
   or   1. . . . Ne4   2. Nf6++;
   or   1. . . . Ne6   2. Nf6++)
57) **1. Qg6   h×g5   2. Q×g7++**
   (or   1. . . . Q×f6   2. Qh7++)
58) **1. Q×f6+   g×f6   2. Bh6++**
   (or   1. . . . Qf7   2. Q×f7++)
59) **1. Q×g6+   f×g6   2. B×f8++**
   (or   1. . . . Kh8   2. Qg7++)
60) **1. g4   Be4   2. Nh4++**
   (or   1. . . . h5   2. B×f5++;
   or   1. . . . h6   2. B×f5++)
61) **1. Qa4+   Kb6   2. Nd5++**
   (or   1. . . . b5   2. Q×b5++)
62) **1. Q×f7+   K×f7   2. B×e6++**
   (or   1. . . . Kh8   2. Qg7++   or   2. Bg7++)
63) **1. b4   Q×g1   R×b7++**
   (other first moves for Black lead to mate by either
   2. B×c5++   or   2. R×b7++)
64) **1. . . . Ng3+   2. f×g3   Qe1++**
   (or   2. hxg3   Qe1++)
65) **1. . . . Qf3+   2. g×f3   Nf2++**
   (or   2. Re2   Q×e2++)
66) **1. . . . Qh3   2. g×h3   N×h3++**
   (if not   2. g×h3, then   2. . . . Q×g2++)
67) **1. . . . Qd1+   2. Q×d1   Ng3++**
   (or   2. Qf1   Q×f1++   or   2. . . . Ng3++)
68) **1. . . . Qg5+   2. f×g5   Bf2++**
   (or   2. Q×g5   Ne2++   or   2. Qg4   Ne2++
   or   2. . . . Q×g4++)
69) **1. . . . Q×f3+   2. g×f3   Bh3++**
   (or   2. Qf2   Q×f2++)
70) **1. . . . Q×f3+   2. K×f3   Nh4++**
   (or   2. Kg1   Qf2++)

71) **1. Qe5 Rg8 2. Qe8+ +**
      (or 1. . . . f6 2. Qe8+ +;
      or 1. . . . Qd8 2. Q×h8+ + or 2. Qg7+ +;
      or 1. . . . g×f5 2. Q×h8+ +;
      or 1. . . . Be7 2. Q×h8+ +;
      or 1. . . . B×e1 2. Qxh8+ +)
72) **1. N×f7+ R×f7 2. Q×g6+ +**
      (or 1. . . . Kh7 2. Q×g6+ +;
      or 1. . . . Kg7 2. Q×g6+ +;
      or 1. . . . Kh5 2. Qh3+ +)
73) **1. Q×h7 R×h7 2. Rf8+ +**
      (or 1. . . . Nf5 2. Q×g6+ +;
      or 1. . . . B×b5 2. Qf7+ + or 2. Qe7+ +;
      or 1. . . . N×f1 2. Qe7+ + or 2. Q×g6+ +;
      or 1. . . . Rc8 2. Qe7+ +)
74) **1. Qe2+ Ra×e2 2. R×a5+ +**
      (or 1. . . . Re×e2 2. R×a7+ +
      or 1. . . . B×e2 2. Bb7+ +
      or 1. . . . Qc4 2. Bb7+ +
      or 1. . . . N×e2 2. b5+ + or 2. Bb7+ +
      or 1. . . . Nb5 2. Q×b5+ + or 2. Bb7+ +)

CHAPTER TWO: MATES IN THREE

75) **1. N×f6+ g×f6 2., Qf7+ Kd7 3. Be6+ +**
      (or 1. . . . Kf8 2. Qf7+ +)
76) **1. Rh8+ K×h8 2. Qh5+ Kg8 3. Qh7+ +**
77) **1. Bf7+ K×f7 2. Ne5+ Ke6 3. Nf7+ +**
      (or 2. . . . Kf8 3. Qf7+ +;
      or 2. . . . Kg8 3. Qf7+ +;
      or 2. . . . Ke6 3. . . . Nc4+ +)
78) **1. Qe8+ K×e8 2. Bb5+ Kd8 3. Re8+ +**
      (or 2. . . . Kf8 3. Re8+ +)
79) **1. Be6+ K×e6 2. Qe8+ Any 3. d5+ +**
80) **1. Qb3+ d5 2. Q×d5+ Q×d5 3. Re8+ +**
      (or 2. . . . Be6 3. Q×e6+ +)

81) **1. Nd2 d6   2. N×e4 d×e5   3. N×f6+ +**
(or   2. . . . N×e4   3. Re8+ +;
or   1. . . . N×d2   2. Rg5+ +)
82) **1. Rh6 g×h6   2. Qg6+ Kh8   3. R×h6+ +**
83) **1. Bh8 Qe5   2. Q×e5 Any   3. Qg7+ +**
84) **1. Be6+ Kc7   2. N×c8+ Qd6   3. Q×d6+ +**
85) **1. Nd7 f5   2. Nef6+ Q×f6   3. N×f6+ +**
(Black is helpless to stop this)
86) **1. N5f6+ g×f6   2. Bh6+ h×g4   3. N×f6+ +**
(or   2. . . . Qg5   3. N×f6+ +;
or   2. . . . Kh7   3. Qg7+ +)
87) **1. Q×h6+ Rg7   2. Qh8+ Rg8   3. Q×g8+ +**
88) **1. Qf5+ g5   2. Q×h7+ Kg4   3. f3+ +**
(or   1. . . . Qg5   2. Q×g5+ +)
89) **1. g7+ Ke7   2. Qe5+ Kf7   3. g×h8/N+ +**
90) **1. R×c7+ Kb8   2. R×b7+ Kc8   3. Nb6+ +**
(or   1. . . . B×c7   2. Q×c7+ +)
91) **1. Qh3+ Ke7   2. Nd5+ Kf8   3. Qh6+ +**
92) **1. Rh4+ Qh5   2. R×h5+ Kg8   3. Nf6+ +**
(or   3. Ne7+ +;
or   1. . . . Kg8   2. Ne7+ +)
93) **1. Q×e6+ f×e6   2. Nb6+ a×b6   3. B×e6+ +**
(or   1. Nb6+ a×b6   2. Q×e6+ f×e6   3. B×e6+ +;
or   2. B×e6+ f×e6   3. Q×e6+ +)
94) **1. R×f6+ g×f6   2. Q×h6+ R×h6   3. B×h6+ +**
(or   2. B×h6+ R×h6   3. Q×h6+ +;
or   1. . . . Qf7   2. Q×f7+ +)
95) **1. Qh4+ Rh5   2. R1f6+ B×f6   3. Q×f6+ +**
(or   1. . . . Kg6   2. Q×h7+ +)
96) **1. Qxe7+ N×e7   2. Nf6+ Kd8   3. N×f7+ +**
(or   2. . . . Kf8   3. Bh6+ +)
97) **1. e5+ K×e5   2. d4+ Kf6   3. Ne4+ +**
(or   1. . . . d×e5   2. Ne4+ +)
98) **1. Nd5+ Ke5   2. Qg7+ K×e6   3. Nf4+ +**
(or   2. . . . Qf6   3. Q×f6+ +)
99) **1. Re1 B×d2   2. Qf3+ Bf4   3. Q×f4+ +**
(or   1. . . . Ne5   2. Q×e5+ +;
or   1. . . . d4   2. . . . Qg5+ +)
100) **1. Qh6+ K×h6   2. Rh4+ Kg7   3. Bh6+ +**

179

101) **1. Qh6 Rg8   2. Q×h7+ K×h7   3. Rh4++**

102) **1. Qf5 Bf4   2. R×f4 Rh8   3. Q×f7++**
(Black cannot cope with the combined attacks against f7 and h7)

103) **1. Q×h7+ K×h7   2. Rh5+ Kg8   3. Rh8++**

104) **1. h5+ Kh6   2. N×e6+ f4   3. Q×g7++**
(or   2. . . . Kh7   3. Q×g7++;
or   2. . . . g5   3. h×g6++)

105) **1. Q×d5+ e×d5   2. Bb6+ Any   3. Re8++**
(or   1. . . . Kc7   2. B×a7++ or   2. Qd6++)

106) **1. Bg6+ h×g6   2. Q×g6+ Any   3. N×e6++**
(or   1. . . . Kf8   2. N×e6++;
or   1. . . . Kd8   2. N×e6++)

107) **1. Qh8+ Ke7   2. Ng6+ f×g6   3. Q×g7++**

108) **1. B×h7+ K×h7   2. Qh5+ Kg8   3. Qh8++**

109) **1. Q×h7+ K×h7   2. Rh4+ Kg8   3. Rh8++**
(or   1. . . . Kf8   2. Qh8++ or   2. Qg7++)

110) **1. Rg8+ K×g8   2. h7+ Kf8   3. h8/Q++**
(or   3. h8/R++)

111) **1. N×e5+ Ng6   2. Q×g6+ Ke7   3. Qf7++**
(or   1. . . . N×h5   2. Bf7++)

112) **1. Nf6+ Q×f6   2. Qd8+ B×d8   3. Bb5++**
(or   1. . . . B×f6   2. Bb5++)

113) **1. Rh8+ B×h8   2. Qh7+ Kf8   3. Q×h8++**
(or   1. . . . K×h8   2. Qh7++;
or   1. . . . Kg7   2. Qh7++)

114) **1. Bh3+ K×g3   2. Ne2+ Kh2   3. Bf1++**

115) **1. Ne5+ N×e5   2. Be8+ Kf8   3. Bg6++**
(or   3. Bh5++)

116) **1. Ba3 f6   2. Qh7+ Kf8   3. Qh8++**
(or   1. . . . g6   2. Qh7+ Kf8   3. Q×f7++
or   3. Qh8++;
or   1. . . . Kf8   2. Qh8++;
or   1. . . . Ng6   2. Qh7++)

117) **1. Qh6+ N×h6   2. B×h6+ Kg8   3. f7++**

118) **1. Be6+ Ke8   2. Q×d8+ K×d8   3. Rc8++**

119) **1. Qf5+ Kh6   2. N×f7+ Any   3. Qg6++**
(or   1. . . . Kh4   2. Nf3+ Kg3   3. Qh3++;
or   3. Qg5++)

120) **1. Ng6+ h×g6   2. Nd5+ e×d5   3. Qe5++**
(or 1. . . . f×g6   2. Bg5++)
121) **1. f8/Q+ B×f8   2. Rf7+ N×f7   3. Re6++**
(or 1. f8/R+, etc.)
122) **1. Qh8+ K×h8   2. N×f7+ Kg8   3. Nh6++**
123) **1. Qh7+ K×h7   2. Rh6+ Kg8   3. Rh8++**
124) **1. Q×h7+ K×h7   2. h×g5+ Any   3. Ne7++**
125) **1. N×g7+ Ke7   2. Nhf5+ R×f5   3. Qe6++**
126) **1. Nf8+ Kh8   2. Qh7+ N×h7   3. Ng6++**
127) **1. Bh7+ Kh8   2. Bg8+ Any   3. Qh7++**
128) **1. Rh8+ B×h8   2. Qh7+ Kf8   3. Q×h8++**
(or 1. . . . K×h8   2. Qh7++)
129) **1. Rh8+ K×h8   2. Qh6+ Kg8   3. Q×g7++**
130) **1. Nf7+ R×f7   2. Ng4+ h×g4   3. Qh1++**
131) **1. Rg4+ f×g4   2. Qf6+ Bg5   3. g3++**
132) **1. Q×h7+ K×h7   2. Rh3+ Kg8   3. Rh8++**
(or 1. . . . Kf8   2. Qh8++)
133) **1. Q×g8+ K×g8   2. Rd8+ Kf7   3. R1d7++**
134) **1. . . . Qh1+   2. K×h1 Ng3+   3. Kg1 Rh1++**
135) **1. . . . Ne2+   2. Kh1 Q×h2+   3. K×h2 Rh5++**
136) **1. . . . Q×f2+   2. R×f2 R×f2+   3. Kh1 Ng3++**
(or 2. Kh1 Ng3++)
137) **1. . . . Rf5+   2. Kg4 h5+   3. Kh3 Rf3++**
138) **1. . . . Q×g1+   2. K×g1 Re8   3. Any Re1++**
139) **1. . . . Nd4+   2. K×d1 Ne3+   3. Kc1 Ne2++**
140) **1. . . . R×h2+   2. K×h2 Q×g3+   3. Kh1 Nf2++**
(or 2. Kg1 Q×g3++)
141) **1. . . . Ne2+   2. Kh1 Ng3+   3. h×g3 h×g5++**
142) **1. . . . Qe3+   2. Kc4 b5+   3. K×c5 Na6++**
143) **1. . . . Ne2   2. K×e2 Bg4+   3. Kd3 Qd4++**
(or 2. Q×e2 Qd4++;
or 2. c4 Qe4++)
144) **1. . . . Bh3+   2. K×h3 Q×f3+   3. Kh4 g5++**
(or 2. Q×h3 Qf2++)
145) **1. . . . R×g2+   2. Kf1 Re2+   3. Kg1 Nf3++**
(or 2. . . . Rg1+   3. K×g1 Nf3++)
146) **1. . . . Qd1+   2. K×d1 R×f1   3. Qe1 Nf2++**
147) **1. . . . Bf1+   2. R×f1 Q×f1+   3. Qg2 Nf2++**
(or 1. . . . Qf1+   2. R×f1 B×f1+   3. Qg2 Nf2++)

148) 1.... Qh3   2. g×h3 Bf3   3. Any N×h3++
149) 1.... Nf3+   2. Q×f3 B×f3+   3. Bg2 Q×g2++
150) 1.... Q×g3+   2. h×g3 Bf3   3. Any Rh1++
    (or   2. Kh1 Bf3++;
     or   2.... Q×h2++;
     or   2.... R×h2++)
151) 1.... R×e2   2. Rg1 B×g2+   3. R×g2 Q×g2++
    (or   2. Q×e2 B×g2++)
152) 1.... Q×d5+   2. K×d5 Be6+   3. Kd6 Ne4++
    (or   3.... Rd8++;
     or   2. Kc3 Rc8++)
153) 1.... Qg3+   2. Qg2 N×f3+   3. Kf1 Qe1++
154) 1.... Ng3+   2. h×g3 Rf1+   3. Kh2 Qg1++
    (or   2. B×g3 Rf1++)
155) 1.... Q×h3   2. Bf7+ Kd8   3. g×h3 g2++
156) 1.... Nd3+   2. e×d3 Q×g3+   3. Ke2 Nd4++
157) 1.... Ng1+   2. R×g1 Bg4+   3. f3 Q×f3++
    (or   2. Kd1 Qc2++)
158) 1.... Q×f2+   2. K×f2 Bc5+   3. Be3 B×e3++
    (or   2. Kh1 Ng3++)
159) 1.... Rd2+   2. N×d2 Nd4+   3. Ke1 Nc2++
160) 1.... Q×g5+   2. K×g5 f6+   3. Kh4 g5++
    (or   3. Kg6 Rh6++)
161) 1.... R×h2+   2. K×h2 Qh4+   3. Kg2 Qh3++
162) 1.... Nd2   2. B×d2 Qh2+   3. Kf1 Q×g2++
163) 1. R×c2+ d×c2   2. Qc3+ Kb5   3. Qc4++;
    (or   1.... Kb5   2. Q×d3+ Ka4   3. Qb3++;
     or   3. Qc4++;
     or   3. Bb3++;
     or   3. Nc3++;
     or   3. Nb6++;
     or   1.... Kd4   2. Rc4++;
     or   2. Q×d3++;
     or   3. Qe3++)
164) 1. Q×g5 R×g5   2. Rf8+ Any   3. R1f7++
    (or   1.... Qd7   2. Q×g8++;
     or   1.... Qg4   2. Qe7++)
165) 1.... Q×f2+   2. K×e4 Bf5+   3. Kd5 Qd4++
    (or   2. Kd3 c4+   3. K×e4 f5++)

166) **1.... Nd5+   2. e×d5 Q×g5+   3. Ke4 Qf4++**
(or   2. N×d5 Q×g5+   3. Nf4 Q×f4++;
or   2. Kd2 Q×g5+   3. Ke1 Rh1++)

167) **1.... Nc2+   2. Kd1 N×f2+   3. Kd2 Bb4++**
(or   2. Kd2 Bb4+   3. Kd1 N×f2++)

168) **1.... R×g3+   2. h×g3 Q×g3+   3. Any Qh2++**
(or   2. Kh1 Rg1+   3. Any Q×h2++)

169) **1. Rb6 Nc5   2. R×c5 a5   3. R×c4++**
(or   1.... a×b6   2. N×b6++;
or   1.... a5   2. Rb4+ a×b4   3. Nb6++)

170) **1.... d5+   2. K×d5 Be6+   3. Kd6 Qe7++**
(or   3. B×e6 Q×e6++;
or   2. N×d5 B×d3++;
or   2. B×d5 B×d3++;
or   2. Kb5 Qa6++)

171) **1.... Nf2+   2. Kh5 g6+   3. Kh6 Bf8++**
(or   2. Kf5 Be4+   3. Ke5 Bf6++;
or   2.... g6+   3. Ke5 Bf6++;
or   2. Kg3 Bh4++)

172) **1.... Bd4   2. N×e7 R×a3+   3. Kb2 Ra2++**
(or   2. d×c3 Q×a3+   3. Kb1 Qa1++
or   3.... Qa2++;
or   2. b4 R×a3+   3. Kb2 Q×b4++)

173) **1. Ng5 N×d3   2. Nf6+ Kh8   3. Nf7++**
(or   2. Ne7+ Kh8   3. Ng6++;
or   1.... Q×g5   2. Nf6+ Kh8   3. Qh7++;
or   1.... Bd6   2. Qh7+ Kf8   3. Qh8++;
or   1.... Ne4   2. Ne7+ Kh8   3. Ng6++;
or   1.... Ne4   2. Nf6+ Kh8   3. Nf7++;
or   1.... g6   2. Q×g6+ Kh8   3. Nf7++
or   3. Qh7++)

174) **1. Ng6 Rg7   2. Qh8+ Kf7   3. Qf8++**
(or   1.... Re8   2. Qh8+ Kf7   3. Qh7++;
or   1.... f5   2. Qh8+ Kf7   3. Ne5++;
or   1.... Rd7   2. Qh8+ Kf7   3. Qf8++
or   2. Qf8+ Kh7   3. Qh8++;
or   1.... Rh7   2. Qf8++;
or   1.... Rf7   2. Qh8++;
or   1.... Kf7   2. Qf8++)

175) **1. N×f7+ Kd7   2. Bf5+ Kc6   3. Nd8+ Kd6   4. Bf4++**
176) **1. Qb3+ d5   2. e×d6+ Be6   3. Q×e6+ Kf8   4. Qf7++**
177) **1. Qd5 Rh7   2. Qg8+ Bf8   3. Ng6+ Any   4. Q×f8++**
178) **1. Nd7 Be7   2. Ne×f6+ B×f6   3. Re8+ Q×e8   4. N×f6++**
179) **1. Qf7+ Kd8   2. Qf8+ Kd7   3. Be6+ K×e6   4. Qf7++**
180) **1. Qb8+ Kd7   2. Nb6+ Ke7   3. Bd6+ Q×d6   4. Q×d6++**
   (or   3. Bd8+ R×d8   4. Q×d8++)
181) **1. Q×f8+ K×f8   2. R×f7+ Kg8   3. Rg7+ Any   4. Rg8++**
182) **1. Rf6+ N×f6   2. R×f6+ Kc5   3. b4+ Kd4   4. c3++**
183) **1. Q×f7+ R×f7   2. Re8+ Bf8   3. Ne7+ N×e7   4. B×f7++**
   (or   2. ... Nf8   3. Ne7++;
   or   2. ... Rf8   3. Ne7++ or   3. Nf6++)
184) **1. g3+ Kh3   2. Qf1+ K×g3   3. Qf2+ Kh3   4. Qh2++**
   (or   1. ... K×g3   2. Qf2+ Kh3   3. Qh2++)
185) **1. Bc4 h6   2. Q×f7+ Kh7   3. Bd3+ f5   4. B×f5++**
   (or   1. ... Q×e6   2. B×e6++)
186) **1. Nd6+ Kd8   2. N×f7+ Ke8   3. Nd6+ Kd8   4. N×e6++**
187) **1. 0-0-0 Nh7   2. Rh1 f5   3. Qg6 Rf7   4. N×f7++**
   (or   1. Ke2 also works)
188) **1. N×b7+ Ke8   2. Q×d7+ K×d7   3. Bb5+ Ke7   4. Rc7++**
   (or   1. Q×d7+ K×d7   2. Bb5+ Ke7   3. Rc7+ Kd8
   4. Rd7++;
   or   2. ... Kd8   3. N×b7+ Ke7   4. Rc7++)
189) **1. Qh5 B×d5   2. R×d5 Q×d5   3. Q×f7+ Q×f7   4. Nd7++**
   (or   4. g3++;
   or   1. ... g6   2. Qh6++)
190) **1. Nf4+ Kf6   2. Qe6+ Kg5   3. Qf5+ Kh4   4. Ng6++**
   (or   1. ... Kf8   2. Ng6++)
191) **1. N×e6+ K×h6   2. Qg7+ Kh5   3. Be2+ Kh4   4. Qg3++**
   (or   3. ... Ng4   4. Qh7++)
192) **1. Qf5+ g5   2. h4 Bd6   3. h×g5+ Bh2   4. R×h2++**
   (or   1. ... Kh4   2. g3++)
193) **1. Q×c6+ N×c6   2. Ra8+ Nd8   3. Bb5+ c6   4. B×c6++**
   (or   2. ... Nb8   3. R×b8++)
194) **1. Qh7+ K×g5   2. h4+ Kg4   3. Q×g7+ Ng6   4. Q×g6++**
   (or   3. ... Kh5   4. Qg5++;
   or   3. ... Kf5   4. Qg5++)

195) **1. Nf6 + Kh8   2. N × f7 + R × f7   3. Rd8 + Rf8   4. R × f8 + +**
196) **1. Rf7 + Kg5   2. f4 + Q × f4   3. e × f4 + Kh4   4. Qf2 + +**
     (or   2. . . . e × f3   3. Q × g6 + +)
197) **1. R × f8 + R × f8   2. Qg7 + K × g7   3. Nf5 + Kg8   4. Nh6 + +**
     (or   1. . . . B × f8   2. Bf7 + +)
198) **1. R × h7 + K × h7   2. Qh1 + Bh4   3. Q × h4 + Kg7**
     4. Qh6 + +
     (or   3. . . . Qh6   4. Q × h6 + +)
199) **1. Qd3 h × g5   2. Qg6 Be5   3. B × e5 Any   4. Q × g7 + +**
     (or   1. . . . Re8   2. Qg6 Be5   3. Q × f7 + Kh8
     4. Q × e8 + +;
     or   1. . . . Rc8   2. Qg6 Be5   3. B × e5 Kf8   4. Q × f7 + +)
200) **1. . . . Qh3   2. f4 Rg6 +   3. Qg4 R × g4 +   4. Kh1 Qg2 + +**
     (or   2. Kh1 Q × h2 + +)
201) **1. . . . Bf3   2. Ne3 B × e3   3. g3 Q × g3 +   4. h × g3 Rh1 + +**
202) **1. . . . R × h2   2. K × h2 Ng4 +   3. Kg1 Qh6   4. Any Qh1 + +**
203) **1. . . . N × c4 +   2. Ke1 Nd3 +   3. Kd1 Qe1 +   4. Any Nf2 + +**
     (or   3. Kf1 Qf2 + +;
     or   2. B × c4 Qf4 + +)
204) **1. . . . Nf2 +   2. Ke1 Nd3 +   3. Kd1 Qe1 +   4. N × e1 Nf2 + +**
     (or   3. Kf1 Qf2 + +)
205) **1. . . . Q × b3   2. a × b3 R × b3   3. Be1 Be3 +   4. Any Rb1 + +**
206) **1. . . . Q × f3 +   2. g × f3 Bh3 +   3. Kg1 Re1 +   4. Kf2 Bh4 + +**
     (or   3. Kf2 Bh4 +   4. Kg1 Re1 + +)
207) **1. . . . Q × h2 +   2. K × h2 Ng3 +   3. Kg1 Rh1 +   4. Kf2**
     R × f1 + +
     (or   2. Kf2 Bh4 + +)
208) **1. . . . Qf1 +   2. Q × f1 B × d4 +   3. Be3 R × e3   4. Kg1 Re1 + +**
     (or   4. Qc4 Re2 + +)
209) **1. . . . Qb5 +   2. Ka3 Qb2 +   3. K × a4 b5 +   4. Ka5 Qa3 + +**
210) **1. . . . Rg2 +   2. Kh1 Rh2 +   3. K × h2 Qf2 +   4. Kh1 Ng3 + +**
     (or   3. Kg1 Qf2 + +;
     or   2. K × g2 Qf2 +   3. Kh1 Ng3 + +)
211) **1. . . . Q × c6 +   2. Qe4 Q × e4 +   3. f3 B × f3 +   4. R × f3**
     Q × f3 + +
     (or   3. . . . Q × f3 +   4. R × f3 B × f3 + +;
     or   2. b × c6 Bf3 + +)
212) **1. . . . R × f2 +   2. Ke3 Bc5 +   3. K × e4 Bf5 +   4. K × e5 Nd7 + +**
213) **1. . . . Q × h3 +   2. N × h3 g4   3. Any R × h3 +   4. Any Rh1 + +**

185

214) 1. ... R×g2+   2. Kh1 Rh2+   3. K×h2 Ng4+   4. Kg1 Bh2++
(or 3. Kg1 Rh1++)
215) 1. ... Rh6   2. Ng3 Qh2+   3. Kf1 Qh1+   4. N×h1 R×h1++
216) 1. N×h6+ g×h6   2. Qg6+ Kh8   3. R×f8+ Qg8   4. R×g8++
(or 4. Q×g8++;
or 1. ... Kh7 2. Nf7+ Kg8 3. Qh8++;
or 2. Nf5+ Kg8 3. Ne7++)
217) 1. R×g7+ Kh8   2. R×h7+ K×h7   3. Qf7+ Kh8   4. Bf6++
(or 3. ... Kh6 4. Rf6++;
or 2. ... Kg8 3. Qf7++;
or 1. ... K×g7 2. Qf7+ Kh6 3. Rf6++;
or 2. ... Kh8 3. Bf6++)
218) 1. R×e6+ Nf6   2. Qe4+ Kh5   3. Be2+ Ng4   4. Q×g4++
(or 2. ... Kf7 3. Re7++;
or 1. ... Q×e6 2. Bd3+ Qe4 3. B×e4++;
or 2. ... Qf5 3. Q×f5++)
219) 1. R×b7+ Rf6   2. Nc6+ Ke8   3. Re7+ Kf8   4. Q×g7++
(or 1. ... h×g5 2. Nc6+ Ke8 3. Re7++)
220) 1. B×g6 f×g6   2. Qe6+ Kf8   3. Qe7+ Kg8   4. Qg7++
(or 1. ... h×g6 2. Qh4 Any 3. Qh8++;
or 1. ... Kf8 2. Bf5, threatening Qg7+ and Qg8++)
221) 1. Nd5+ e×d5+   2. B×f6+ Kd6   3. Be5+ Ke7   4. Bd6++
(or 1. ... N×d5 2. Qh7+ Bg7 3. Q×g7++)
222) 1. Nf8+ B×f8   2. Q×c2+ Rf5   3. Q×f5+ Kg7   4. Qg6++
(or 1. ... R×f8 2. B×c2+ Rf5 3. B×f5++)
223) 1. ... Ng1+   2. Ke1 Qd1+   3. K×d1 Rf1+   4. Qe1 Nf2++
(or 2. h×g4 Rf1+ 3. Qe1 Nf2++)
224) 1. ... Ne4+   2. Ke3 N×c2+   3. Kd3 N×b4+
4. K×e4   Qd4++
(or 3. K×e4 Qd4++;
or 2. Ke1 N×c2++;
or 2. Kg1 Nf3++ or 2. ... Ne2++)
225) 1. ... Bb4+   2. Ke3 e×f4+   3. K×d4 Qf6+   4. e5 Q×e5++
(or 2. c3 Qf2 + 3. Qe2 Q×e2++)
226) 1. ... Rd6   2. Qd2 g5   3. Q×g5 B×g5   4. Any Rh6++
(or 3. Q×d6 g4++;
or 2. Qe4 Rh6+ 3. Qh4 g5 4. Q×h6 g4++;
or 2. Qe4 Rh6+ 3. Qh4 g5 4. g4 R×h4++)

227) **1. . . . Q×c1   2. Re1 Rf1+   3. R×f1 R×f1+   4. Q×f1   Q×f1++**
(or   2. Q×c1 Rf1+   3. Q×f1 R×f1++)

228) **1. Ba5+ Nc7   2. B×c7+ Q×c7   3. Q×c7+ Ke8   3. Nd6++**
(or   4. Bd7++;
or   1. . . . Qb6   2. Qd6+ Ke8   3. Qd7++;
or   1. . . . Ke8   2. Nd6++)

229) **1. Bf8+ Kc7   2. Rd7+ Kb8   3. Re8+ Qc8   4. Bd6++**
(or   1. . . . Kc8   2. Re8+ Kc7   3. Rd7++;
or   1. . . . Qd7   2. R×d7+ Kc8   3. Re8++)

230) **1. h5+ N×h5   2. Q×h5+ Kf6   3. Nce4+ Kf5   4. g4++**
(or   2. . . . Kf5   3. g4+ Kf6   4. Nce4++;
or   1. . . . K×g5   2. e4++;
or   1. . . . Kf5   2. e4+ N×e4   3. Qf3++)

231) **1. B×c5+ Kf6   2. e5+ Kg6   3. Q×g4+ Kh6   4. Qg5++**
(or   2. . . . Kf5   3. Bc2+ Qe4   4. Q×e4++;
or   1. . . . R×c5   2. Q×c5+ Kf6   3. Qg5++)

232) **1. . . . Bf5+   2. Kf3 Nd4+   3. Kg2 Bh3+   4. Kg1 Q×e1++**
(or   3. Ke3 Qf4++;
or   2. Ke3 Qf4+   3. Ke2 Bg4+   4. Bf3 Q×f3++;
or   2. Ke3 Qf4+   3. Ke2 Bg4+   4. Kd3 Qd4++;
or   2. K×f5 Qf4+   3. Ke6 Qf6++)

CHAPTER FOUR: MATES IN FIVE

233) **1. g×f7+ R×f7   2. B×f7+ Kf8   3. Rh8+ Ke7   4. Nd5+ Kd6   5. Nc4++**

234) **1. R×h7+ Kg8   2. Qh5 B×f2+   3. Kf1 Kf8   4. Rh8+ Bg8 5. R×g8++**

235) **1. Qd4 B×f2+   2. K×f2 Qc2+   3. Kg1 Qg6   4. B×g6 Any 5. Q×g7++**

236) **1. Qe6+ Kh8   2. Nf7+ Kg8   3. Nh6+ Kh8   4. Qg8+ Any 5. Nf7++**
(or   1. . . . Kf8   2. Qf7++)

237) **1. Qd5+ Kc8 2. Qd7+ Kb8 3. Qd8+ Nc8 4. Q×c8+ K×c8 5. Re8++**
(or 1. . . . N×d5 2. Re8++)

238) **1. Qd7+ B×d7 2. Nd6+ Kd8 3. Nf7+ Kc8 4. Re8+ B×e8 5. Rd8++**

239) **1. N×f5+ g×f5 2. Qh3+ Kg6 3. Qg3+ Kh6 4. Bg7+ Kh5 5. Be2++**
(or 1. . . . Kh5 2. Be2++)

240) **1. Bh7+ Kh8 2. Bg6+ Kg8 3. Rh8+ K×h8 4. Qh2+ Kg8 5. Qh7++**

241) **1. Qh6+ Kg8 2. Nf6+ Kf7 3. Qh7+ Ke6 4. Qg8+ Ke5 5. Qd5++**
(or 4. . . . Ke7 5. Qe8++;
or 3. . . . Kf8 4. Qg8+ Ke7 5. Qe8++)

242) **1. Ne6+ d×e6 2. Rd1+ Qd2 3. R×d2+ Nd4 4. R×d4+ Bd7 5. Q×d7++**

243) **1. Qf5+ Kc7 2. Qc8+ Kb6 3. Q×b7+ Ka5 4. Nc4+ Ka4 5. Qb3++**
(or 5. b3++;
or 2. . . . K×d6 3. Bf4++;
or 1. . . . K×d6 2. Bf4++;
or 1. . . . Kd8 2. Qc8++)

244) **1. Bd6+ K×d6 2. Qc5+ Ke6 3. d5+ Ke5 4. d6+ K×e4 5. Nd2++**
(or 4. . . . Ke6 5. Qd5++;
or 1. . . . Ke6 2. Qd5++)

245) **1. Rg7+ Kh5 2. Bf7+ K×h4 3. Kh2 Be1 4. g3+ B×g3+ 5. B×g3++**
(or 1. . . . Kf5 2. Rf1++)

246) **1. N×c8+ Kg8 2. Ne7+ Kf8 3. Ng6+ Kg8 4. Qf8+ Any 5. Ne7++**
(or 1. . . . N×c5 2. Rd8++;
or 1. . . . Ke8 2. Qe7++)

247) **1. B×h7+ N×h7 2. Nh6+ g×h6 3. Qg6+ Bg7 4. Qf7+ Kh8 5. Ng6++**
(or 3. . . . Kh8 4. Nf7++;
or 3. . . . Kf8 4. Qf7++;
or 2. . . . Kf8 3. Ng6++;
or 2. . . . Kh8 3. Ng6++;
or 1. . . . Kh8 2. Nf7++)

188

248) 1. Q×g7+ K×g7   2. Rg3+ Kh6   3. Bc1+ Kh5   4. Be2+
K×h4   5. Rh3++
249) 1. Q×f7+ Kh8   2. Qh5+ Kg8   3. Qh7+ Kf8   4. Qh8+ Ke7
5. Q×g7++
250) 1. Qe6 N×e6   2. Ng6+ h×g6   3. Rh3+ Kg8   4. B×e6+
Kf8   5. Rh8++
(or   2. . . . Kg8   3. B×e6++)
251) 1. Qd5+ Kg6   2. Qg5+ Kf7   3. Qf5+ Bf6   4. Ng5+ Kg8
5. Q×h7++
(or   3. . . . Kg8   4. Q×f8++)
252) 1. Qd3+ Kh5   2. g4+ K×g4   3. f3+ Kg3   4. Rh3+ Kg2
5. Qf1++
(or   3. . . . Kh5   4. Qh7++)
253) 1. Nc3 b×c3   2. a4 Qc4   3. Q×c4 b6   4. Bc8+ Ka5
5. Q×b5++
254) 1. Qd6+ Ka8   2. R×a7+ K×a7   3. Ra1+ Ba6   4. Qc7+
Qb7   5. R×a6++
255) 1. R×f7+ K×f7   2. Qg6+ Kf8   3. Rf1+ Qf6   4. R×f6+
g×f6   5. Q×f6++
(or   4. . . . Ke7   5. Q×g7++ or   5. Qf7++
or   5. Rf7++)
256) 1. h7+ K×h7   2. Be4+ Kg8   3. Rg1+ Qg3+   4. R×g3+
Ng5   5. R×g5++
(or   4. . . . Ng7   5. Q×g7++)
257) 1. . . . Rf8+   2. Kg1 Rf2   3. Ng6+ h×g6   4. d6+ c×d6
5. Any Nf3++
258) 1. . . . Q×h3+   2. K×h3 Ne3+   3. Be6 B×e6+   4. Kh4
Nf3+   5. Kh5 Bg4++
(or   4. . . . Ng6+   5. Kh5 Bg4++;
or   2. Kg1 Nf3++)
259) 1. . . . Q×b2+   2. K×c4 Ba6+   3. K×c5 Qb4+   4. Kc6
Qb5+   5. Kd6 Qd5++
(or   2. Ka4 Qb4++)
260) 1. . . . Bf3   2. g×f3 g×f3   3. Kg1 Qh8   4. Bh4 R×h4   5. Any
Rh1++
261) 1. . . . Qh2+   2. Kf1 R×e3   3. f×e3 B×h3+   4. Ke1 Bg3+
5. Qf2 Q×f2++

262) **1. Qh5+ Ke7   2. Qf7+ Kd6   3. e5+ f×e5   4. Qd5+ Ke7**
5. Q×e5++
(or   3. . . . Kc6   4. Qd5+ Kb6   5. Qb5++;
or   3. . . . Kc5   4. Qd5+ Kb4   5. Qb5++;
or   4. . . . Kb6   5. Qb5++;
or   3. . . . K×e5   4. Qd5++)

263) **1. h5+ Kh6   2. Q×f4+ Kg7   3. Qf7+ Kh6   4. d4+ Qg5**
5. Q×f8++
(or   4. d3+ Qg5   5. Q×f8++;
or   2. . . . Qg5   3. Q×f8+ Qg7   4. d3++;
or   4. d4++)

264) **1. Qa3+ Kf6   2. Qc3+ Kf5   3. Qe5+ Kg4   4. f3+ Kh4**
5. Bg3++
(or   2. . . . Ke7   3. Qc5+ Kf6   4. Bg5++;
or   2. . . . e5   3. Q×e5++)

265) **1. Nf7+ Kg8   2. Ne5+ Nc4   3. B×c4+ Kh8   4. Ng6+**
h×g6   5. Rh4++
(or   3. . . . Rf7   4. Rd8++;
or   1. . . . R×f7   2. Rd8+ Rf8   3. R×f8++)

266) **1. Qg7+ K×g7   2. Rf×f7+ Kg8   3. Rg7+ Kh8   4. Rh7+**
Kg8   5. Rbg7++
(or   2. . . . Kh6   3. Rh7++)

267) **1. . . . N×e4+   2. Ke2 Qf2+   3. Kd3 Nc5+   4. Kc4 Qd4+**
5. Kb5 Qb4++
(or   5. . . . a6++;
or   2. Ke3 Qf2+   3. Kd3 Nc5+, etc.;
or   3. K×e4 Bf5++)

268) **1. . . . Q×d4+   2. Kd2 Qe3+   3. Kc3 Bg7+   4. e5 B×e5+**
5. Kc4 Qd4++
(or   2. . . . K×d4 Bg7+   3. e5 B×e5+   4. Ke4 Nf6++;
or   4. . . . f5++;
or   3. Kc4 Ba6++ or   3. . . . Be6++)

269) **1. . . . Nf3+   2. Kh1 Qd6   3. g3 Rh5   4. h4 R×h4+   5. g×h4**
Qh2++
(or   5. Kg2 Rh2++;
or   3. g×f3 B×f3+   4. Kg1 Rg5++;
or   2. g×f3 Rg5+   3. Kh1 B×f3++;
or   2. g×f3 Qg5+   3. Kh1 B×f3++)

270) **1. Nf6 + Kh6   2. N × g4 + Kh5   3. Qh3 + Kg6   4. Ne5 + Kf6**
5. Rf7 + +
> (or   5. Re6 + + or   5. Qe6 + +;
> or   1. . . . g × f6   2. R × h7 + R × h7   3. Q × h7 + +;
> or   1. . . . Kh4   2. Bg3 + + or   2. Qg3 + +)

271) **1. Qg4 + K × e5   2. d4 + K × d4   3. Be3 + K × e3   4. Rad1**
B × g4   5. Rd3 + +
> (or   3. . . . Kc4   4. Qe2 + Kb4   5. Qb5 + +;
> or   1. . . . Ke7   2. Q × g7 + Ke6   3. Qf7 + K × e5
> 4. Qd5 + +;
> or   2. . . . Ke8   3. Qf7 + +)

272) **1. Qh5 + Ke7   2. Qf7 + Kd6   3. e5 + f × e5   4. Qd5 + Ke7**
5. Q × e5 + +
> (or   3. . . . K × e5   4. Re4 + Kd6   5. Qd5 + +;
> or   4. . . . Kf5   5. Qh5 + +;
> or   3. . . . Kc6   4. Qd5 + Kb6   5. Qb5 + +;
> or   3. . . . Kc5   4. Qd5 + Kb4   5. Qb5 + +)

273) **1. Nf6 + Kh8   2. Qh5 g × f6   3. Rh3 h6   4. Q × h6 + Kg8**
5. Qh7 + +
> (or   5. Qh8 + +;
> or   5. Rg3 + +;
> or   2. . . . h6   3. Q × f7 Any   4. Ng6 + +;
> or   1. . . . g × f6   2. Qg4 + Kh8   3. Rg3 and mate next
> move at g7 or g8)

274) **1. N × e6 + f × e6   2. Q × h6 + Kf7   3. B × g6 + Ke7   4. Qg7 +**
Rf7   5. Q × f7 + +
> (or   3. . . . Kg8   4. Qh7 + +;
> or   2. . . . Kh8   3. B × g6 + Kg8   4. Qh7 + +;
> or   1. . . . B × e6   2. Q × h6 + Kh8   3. B × g6 + Kg8
> 4. Qh7 + +;
> or   1. . . . Kh8   2. Q × h6 B × c3 +   3. b × c3 f × e6
> 4. B × g6 + Kg8   5. Qh7 + +;
> or   3. . . . Qf6   4. B × g6 + Kg8   5. Qh7 + +;
> or   3. . . . Rg8   4. B × g6 + +)

275) **1. Qd6+ Kc8 2. Be6+ Qd7 3. B×d7+ Kd8 4. Be6+ Ke8 5. Qd7+ Kf8 6. Qf7++**

276) **1. e×f7+ Kd7 2. Be6+ Kc6 3. Ne5+ Kb5 4. Bc4+ Ka5 5. Bb4+ Ka4 6. a×b3++**
    (or 4. . . . Ka4 5. a×b3+ Ka5 6. Bb4++)

277) **1. Qh4+ Kg6 2. Qh7+ K×g5 3. h4+ Kg4 4. Q×g7+ Ng6 5. Q×g6+ Qg5 6. Q×g5++**
    (or 4. . . . Kh5 5. Qg5++;
    or 4. . . . Kf5 5. Qg5++)

278) **1. Qh6+ K×h6 2. Nhf5+ B×f5 3. N×f5+ Kh5 4. g4+ K×g4 5. Rg3+ Kh5 6. Be2++**

279) **1. Bh7+ Kh8 2. Bg6+ Kg8 3. Rh8+ K×h8 4. Qh1+ Qh4 5. Q×h4+ Kg8 6. Qh7++**

280) **1. B×f7+ K×f7 2. Qd5+ Ke8 3. f7+ Ke7 4. Re1+ Qe5 5. Bg5+ Nf6 6. R×e5++**
    (or 2. . . . K×f6 3. Bg5++)

281) **1. B×f7+ K×f7 2. Ng5+ Ke8 3. Qe6 Bd5 4. R×d5 Qd6 5. R×d6 Rd8 6. Qf7++**
    (or 4. . . . Qf4 5. Qd7++;
    or 2. . . . Kf6 3. Qe6++)

282) **1. Qh6+ Kf7 2. Ng5+ Ke7 3. Qg7+ Kd6 4. Qd7+ Ke5 5. Q×e6+ Kf4 6. Nh3++**
    (or 3. . . . Kd8 4. Qd7++;
    or 1. . . . Ke7 2. Qg7+ Kd8 3. Qd7++;
    or 2. . . . Kd6 3. Qd7++)

283) **1. . . . Rg2+ 2. Kf1 R×d2+ 3. Kg1 Rg2+ 4. Kf1 Ra2+ 5. Kg1 R×a1+ 6. Bc1 R×c1++**

284) **1. . . . Rh1+ 2. K×h1 Qh8+ 3. Kg1 N×g4 4. B×g5+ Kf8 5. Be7+ K×e7 6. Any Qh2++**

285) **1. . . . Nb4+ 2. Kc4 N×d2+ 3. Kb5 a6+ 4. Ka5 b6+ 5. Ka4 N×c2+ 6. b4 Q×b4++**
    (or 6. Be4 Q×e4 and mates as above;
    or 6. Bc4 Q×c4 and mates as above)

286) **1. . . . Ne2+ 2. Kh1 Q×f2 3. Q×g7+ K×g7 4. Bb2+ Kg8 5. Nc3 Qg1+ 6. R×g1 Nf2++**

287) 1. . . . Nf×d4+   2. c×d4 N×d4+   3. Kc3 Bb4+   4. K×b4
Nc6+   5. Kb3 Qb4+   6. Kc2 Nd4++
      (or   5. Kc3 Qb4+   6. Kc2 Nd4++;
       or   5. Ka3 Qb4++;
       or   5. Kb5 Qb4++)

288) 1. Nc7+ Ke7   2. Q×f7+ Kd6   3. Bf4+ Ne5   4. B×e5+
Kc6   5. Qc4+ Bc5   6. Qb5++
      (or   5. . . . Kd7   6. Qe6++;
       or   5. . . . Kb6   6. Qb5++;
       or   3. . . . Kc6   4. Qd5+ Kb6   5. Qb5++;
       or   1. . . . Q×c7   2. Q×f7+ Kd8   3. Ne6++)

289) 1. . . . Qf2+   2. K×e4 d5+   3. Kd3 e4+   4. Kc3 Qd4+   5. Kb3
Q×c4+   6. Ka3 Qb4++
      (or   3. . . . Bf5+   4. Kc3 Qd4+   5. Kb3 Q×c4+   6. Ka3
      Qb4++;
       or   3. B×d5 Bf5++;
       or   3. K×d5 Qd4++;
       or   2. Kd3 Nc5+   3. Kc3 Qd4++)

290) 1. . . . Rb1+   2. Ka4 Bd7+   3. Ka5 Bd8+   4. K×a6 Bc8+
5. Ka7 Bb6+   6. Kb8 Ba6++
      (or   6. Ka8 Ba6++;
       or   3. Nb5 B×b5+   4. Ka5 Bd8++)

291) 1. . . . Ba6+   2. Kf3 Qf6+   3. Bf4 Nh4+   4. Kg4 Bc8+   5. Kh5
g6+   6. Kh6 Qg7++
      (or   6. . . . Nf5++;
       or   3. Kg4 Bc8+   4. Kh5 Qg5++)

292) 1. . . . R×h2+   2. K×h2 Qh4+   3. Nh3 B×h3   4. Rf2
Bg4+   5. Kg1 Q×f2+   6. Kh2 Qh4++
      (or   4. g×h3 Qg3+   5. Kh1 Q×h3++)

293) 1. . . . Qe1+   2. Rf1 Q×e3+   3. Kh1 Nf2+   4. Kg1 Nh3+
5. Kh1 Qg1+   6. R×g1 Nf2++
      (or   4. R×f2 Qe1+   5. Rf1 Q×f1++;
       or   3. Rf2 Q×f2+   4. Kh1 Qf1++)

193

294) 1. ... R×f1+   2. K×f1 Rf8+   3. Bf4 R×f4+   4. Ke2
Qe3+   5. Kd1 Rf1+   6. Kc2 B×e4++
(or   4. Kg1 Rf2   5. Any Q×g2++;
or   3. Ke2 Rf2+   4. Kd1 Qd3+   5. Bd2 Q×d2++;
or   3. Ke2 Rf2+   4. Kd1 Qd3+   5. Ke1 Rf1++;
or   3. Ke2 Rf2+   4. Ke1 Q×g2   5. Any Qf1++;
or   3. Kg1 Rf2   4. Any Q×g2++)

295) 1. ... Rd3+   2. K×b4 R×b3+   3. Kc5 Rd8   4. Bf4 b6+
5. Kc6 Rd4   6. Any Bd7++
(or   5. ... Rd3   6. Any Bd7++;
or   3. Ka5 Bc4   4. Any b6++)

296) 1. Bc5+ Ka6   2. Qf1+ b5   3. a4 c6   4. Q×b5+ c×b5
5. a×b5+ K×b5   6. c4++
(or   2. ... Ka5   3. b4+ Ka4   4. Bb3++;
or   1. ... Ka5   2. b4+ Ka4   3. c4 Any
4. Nec3++;
or   1. ... Ka5   2. b4+ Kb5   3. Qf1+ Ka4   4. Bb3++;
or   1. ... Kb5   2. Qf1+ Ka4   3. Qc4+ Ka5   4. Qb4+
Ka6   5. Qa4++;
or   1. ... Kb5   2. Qf1+ Ka5   3. b4+ Ka4   4. Bb3++)

297) 1. c5 a5   2. Rab1 Q×h2+   3. K×h2 Rh6+   4. Kg1 Rh1+
5. K×h1 Any   6. Ba6++
(or   1. ... e5   2. Ba6+ Kb8   3. Rd8+ Qc8
4. R×c8++;
or   1. ... Kb7   2. Rab1+ Ka8   3. Rd8++;
or   1. ... Rg8   2. Rab1, and Black can only delay
5. Ba6++)

298) 1. ... Nf3+   2. g×f3 Qd4+   3. Kg2 Qf2+   4. Kh3 Q×f3+
5. Kh4 Nh6   6. Rg1 Nf5+   6. Kg5 Qh5++

299) 1. ... R×h2+   2. K×h2 Rh8+   3. Kg3 Nh5+   4. Kh4
Nf4+   5. Kg3 Rg8+   6. Kh2 R×g2+   7. Kh1 Qh5++
(or   6. K×f4 Qg5++;
or   6. Kh4   Qh5++;
or   5. Kg4 Rg8+   6. K×f4 Qg5++;
or   4. Kg4 Qf5+   5. Kh4 Qf4+   6. g4 Ng7++;
or   6. Kh3 Ng7++)

194

300) 1. N×g7+ Kf8   2. Ne6+ f×e6   3. Qh6+ Ke8   4. Bg6+
h×g6   5. Q×h8+ Kf7   6. Qg7+ Ke8   7. Qe7++
(or 3. . . . Kf7   4. Qg7+ Ke8   5. Qe7++;
or 3. . . . Kg8   4. Qg7++;
or 2. . . . Ke8   3. Nc7+ Kf8   4. Qh6+ Kg8
5. Qg7++;
or 2. . . . Kg8   3. Qg5++;
or 2. . . . B×e6   3. Qd8++)

INDEX

About the Author

BRUCE PANDOLFINI is the author of thirteen instructional chess books, including *Chessercizes, Bobby Fischer's Outrageous Chess Moves, Principles of the New Chess, Pandolfini's Endgame Course, Russian Chess, The ABC's of Chess, Let's Play Chess, Kasparov's Winning Chess Tactics, One-Move Chess by the Champions, Chess Openings: Traps and Zaps, Square One,* and *Weapons of Chess.* He is also the editor of the distinguished anthologies *The Best of Chess Life & Review,* Volumes I and II. Perhaps the most experienced chess teacher in North America, co-founder with Faneuil Adams of the Manhattan Chess Club School and director of the New York City Schools Program, Bruce Pandolfini lives in Manhattan.